TWENTIETH CENTURY VIEWS

The aim of this series is to present the best in contemporary critical opinion on major authors, providing a twentieth century perspective on their changing status in an era of profound revaluation.

Maynard Mack, *Series Editor*
Yale University

EARLY AMERICAN LITERATURE

A COLLECTION OF CRITICAL ESSAYS

Edited by

Michael T. Gilmore

Prentice-Hall, Inc. A SPECTRUM BOOK *Englewood Cliffs, N.J.*

Library of Congress Cataloging in Publication Data
Main entry under title:

Early American literature.

(Twentieth century views) (A Spectrum Book)

Bibliography: p.

1. American literature—Colonial period, ca. 1600-1775—History and criticism—Addresses, essays, lectures.
2. American literature—Revolutionary period, 1775-1783—History and criticism—Addresses, essays, lectures.
3. American literature—1783-1850—History and criticism—Addresses, essays, lectures.   I. Gilmore, Michael T.

PS185.E2   810'.9'001   80-17853

ISBN 0-13-222513-1

ISBN 0-13-222463-1 (pbk.)

Editorial/production supervision by Betty Neville
Cover design by Vivian Berger. © 1980 by Vivian Berger
Manufacturing buyer: Barbara A. Frick

10   9   8   7   6   5   4   3   2   1

PRENTICE-HALL INTERNATIONAL, INC. *(London)*
PRENTICE-HALL OF AUSTRALIA, PTY. LTD. *(Sydney)*
PRENTICE-HALL OF CANADA, LTD. *(Toronto)*
PRENTICE-HALL OF INDIA PRIVATE LIMITED *(New Delhi)*
PRENTICE-HALL OF JAPAN, INC. *(Tokyo)*
PRENTICE-HALL OF SOUTHEAST ASIA PTE. LTD. *(Singapore)*
WHITEHALL BOOKS LIMITED *(Wellington, New Zealand)*

For Debbie

Contents

Introduction
by Michael T. Gilmore   1

Captain John Smith's Image of America
by Edwin C. Rozwenc   11

A Colonial Dialect
by Perry Miller   22

Puritan Poetics
by Robert Daly   34

Israel in Babylon:
The Archetype of the Captivity Narratives
by Richard Slotkin   46

The Garden of the Chattel:
Robert Beverley and William Byrd II
by Lewis P. Simpson   62

Jonathan Edwards and Typology
by Ursula Brumm   70

The *Autobiography* of Benjamin Franklin
by Robert F. Sayre   84

Whig Sentimentalism
by Kenneth Silverman   98

Common Sense and Paine's Republicanism
by Eric Foner   105

Thomas Jefferson and the Equality of Man
by Garry Wills   121

"The Double-Tongued Deceiver":
Sincerity and Duplicity
in the Novels of Charles Brockden Brown
by Michael Davitt Bell   133

The Image of America:
From Hermeneutics to Symbolism
    by Sacvan Bercovitch   159

The Colonial Experience
in the Literature of the United States
    by Kenneth B. Murdock   168

Chronology of Important Dates   *177*
Notes on the Editor and Contributors   *180*
Selected Bibliography   *182*

Introduction

by Michael T. Gilmore

The past few years have seen a dramatic growth of interest in early American literature, both as a field of study in its own right and as a vital source of influence on subsequent patterns of American thought. The essays in this volume should help to illuminate some of the reasons for that interest by providing a critical introduction to the richness and diversity of American culture in its formative stages. The period covered by the essays extends from the earliest English settlement at Jamestown to the turn of the eighteenth century, and the topics discussed range from the Puritan plain style through the captivity narrative to the beginnings of the American novel. Along the way there are detailed considerations of such major authors as Jonathan Edwards, Benjamin Franklin, Thomas Paine, and Thomas Jefferson. It seems quite futile, given this variety, to attempt to identify a unifying thread or dominant theme in the literature of early America. Nevertheless, before the reader turns to the individual essays, it may be helpful to review two developments in recent scholarship that have greatly increased understanding of the period and have far-reaching implications for American cultural and literary history.

I

For literary purposes perhaps the more important of these developments has been the recovery of millennialism as a central component of Puritan thought. This aspect of the "New England mind" has been thoroughly documented in the last decade, and it is now apparent that the Puritan migration to the wilderness was fraught with apocalyptic expectations from the very start. Indeed, as Sacvan Bercovitch and others have shown, the Puritan colonists believed that the New Jerusalem would be established in

America. They arrived at this belief from their typological reading of the Scriptures, which encouraged them to view world history as the progressive unfolding of God's plan for his chosen people. In their minds the Bible *was* the book of history, and typology revealed the developmental pattern of events by finding correspondences between the Old and New Testaments. Jonah, for example, was a "type" or foreshadowing of Christ, his three days in the belly of the whale a prefiguration of the Savior's three days in the tomb. Similarly, the ancient Hebrews were a type of the Christian elect, whose redemption at the end of time had been foretold in the book of Revelation. In the seventeenth century many English Puritans became persuaded that the Johannine prophecy of a heavenly kingdom on earth for God's new Israel was about to be realized. The New Englanders not only shared this conviction but, by interpreting their own role in history typologically, they concluded that the millennial promises applied directly to themselves. Their earliest writings express their faith that they were latter-day Israelites who had been summoned from the English Egypt to take possession of a second Promised Land.

Illustrations of this apocalyptic mentality are extremely plentiful throughout the entire Puritan era, from the founding of Massachusetts Bay to the decline of the theocracy. When John Winthrop addressed the emigrant Puritans in 1630, he declared that "the God of Israel is among us" and assured his listeners that they would be an example to all mankind—"a city upon a hill." Edward Johnson, who wrote a history of New England in 1653, was confident that "this is the place where the Lord will create a new Heaven, and a new Earth." And almost half a century later Cotton Mather paused in his account of the witchcraft episode to speculate that Satan's raging against the New English Israel proved "the *Thousand Years* is not very *Far Off.*"

Millennialism did not die out with Puritanism, moreover. Although confidence in New England's historic destiny seems to have waned by the end of the seventeenth century, apocalyptic fervor revived during the Great Awakening and contributed to the growth of American nationalism. Jonathan Edwards, the foremost American awakener, gave new life to the Puritan idea of communal election when he interpreted the revival in the colonies as the dawn of the millennial age. According to Edwards, "the Sun of Righteousness" then rising in the west would shine forth from America until it regenerated the human race. (As Ursula Brumm points out in her essay on Edwards, he used typological proofs in support of his claim that America would redeem the sins of Europe. It might be argued in fact that he was making a novel extension of typological method to geography. Strictly speaking, typology has to do with the temporal sequence of the two testaments; but Edwards, in his vision of the imminent millennium, implied that the New *World* — where Christ would reign in spirit — was the typological fulfillment of the Old, which "hath slain Christ and...shed the blood of the saints and martyrs of Jesus...." Writers of the Revolutionary period emphasized liberty rather than piety, but they too believed that America had a special role to play in history. John Adams commented in the year of the Stamp Act crisis that the "settlement of America" had marked "the Opening of a grand scene and design in Providence, for the Illumination of...Mankind over all the Earth." To the Connecticut clergyman Samuel Sherwood, the struggle with Britain provided confirmation that "God Almighty, with all the powers of heaven, are on our side." Even Thomas Paine was moved to speak in apocalyptic phrases when he called his adopted countrymen to arms in 1776: "We have it in our power to begin the world over again...The birthday of a new world is at hand."

The successful outcome of the Revolution made millennialism an article of patriotic faith for many Americans, who continued into the next century and beyond to proclaim the United States as the world's "redeemer nation." The extraordinary persistence of this idea can be seen not only in public discourse but in the literature of American romanticism. D. H. Lawrence, in his study of American writers from Franklin to Whitman, sensed the enduring power of the millennial creed when he remarked that to "the true American" the nation is not a "blood-home-land" but a "spirit-home-land," "a universal idea" rather than "a local thing." This was quite literally true for the early Melville, who sounds in his novel *White-Jacket* like a latter-day Puritan:

> We Americans are the peculiar, chosen people — the Israel of our time; we bear the ark of the liberties of the world. ...God has pre-

destined, mankind expects, great things from our race; and great
things we feel in our souls.... And let us always remember that with
ourselves...national selfishness is unbounded philanthropy, for
we cannot do a good to America, but we give alms to the world.

The attraction of apocalyptic themes for the literary imagination is not confined to overt statements of American exceptional-
ism. Other writers who do not share the youthful Melville's
nationalistic sentiments turn the apocalyptic tradition to their
own imaginative purposes by continuing to employ prophetic
language and symbolism. In *Walden,* for example, Thoreau presents himself as a kind of nineteenth-century "great awakener,"
bragging "as lustily as chanticleer in the morning...to wake my
neighbors up." Although he doubts that "John or Jonathan" will
understand him — meaning, it seems, not only England (John Bull)
and America but St. John the Divine and Jonathan Edwards — he
trusts that his crowing will awaken the reader to the "morning
star," a phrase used in the book of Revelation to refer to Christ
in his second coming. Even so alienated a writer as Poe, who in
many ways seems scarcely American at all, assimilates elaborate
millennial imagery into his personal and highly unorthodox
cosmology. Poe has a particular fondness for motifs from Revelation: in the apocalyptic timetable of "The Fall of the House of
Usher," the slaying of a dragon is correlated with Lady Made-
leine's rising from the tomb. Moreover, the tale itself ends with
the destruction of the house and can accordingly be read as the
conclusion to Roderick Usher's poem "The Haunted Palace,"
which describes in six stanzas the Edenic origins and gradual
disintegration of his world. In this way the story is made to correspond with the seventh and climactic stage of history as envisioned in Revelation.

II

A second notable development in recent scholarship on early
America has been the reassessment of eighteenth-century republi-
canism by historians like Bernard Bailyn, Gordon S. Wood, and
J. G. A. Pocock. These and other scholars have shown that Anglo-
American political thought was long dominated by an ideological

division known as the "Court-Country" controversy. Considered from one perspective, the confrontation between the Court and Country may be understood as a quarrel between the supporters and opponents of the new economic order of financial capitalism. The Country position (also called "Real Whig" or "Commonwealth") was identified with the critics of governmental policy in England, and during the Revolutionary period it supplied many of the ideas and arguments with which the colonists advanced their own cause against the Crown. After independence the Court-Country conflict was revived in the United States by the Hamiltonians and the Jeffersonians as they joined debate over the economic and political future of the new republic. The primary importance of this debate for literary and cultural studies would seem to lie in the emphasis it placed on the relationship between property and freedom.

It is well known that the Jeffersonians advocated an agrarian commonwealth and regarded ownership of land or real property as the foundation of republican virtue. Jefferson himself spelled out his views on this matter in a famous passage from the *Notes on the State of Virginia*. "Those who labor in the earth," he wrote,

> are the chosen people of God, if ever he had a chosen people, whose breasts he has made his peculiar deposit for substantial and genuine virtue. It is the focus in which he keeps alive that sacred fire, which otherwise might escape from the face of the earth. Corruption of morals in the mass of cultivators is a phenomenon of which no age nor nation has furnished an example. It is the mark of those who, not looking up to heaven, to their own soil and industry, as does the husbandman, for their subsistence, depend for it on the casualties and caprice of customers. Dependence begets subservience and venality, suffocates the germ of virtue, and prepares fit tools for the designs of ambition.

In this formulation, only the husbandman is said to possess the economic independence necessary for freedom. His integrity is incorruptible because he relies solely on his "own soil and industry" to support himself; he is not subject to the wills of other men. Somewhat anachronistically, land is seen here as conferring self-sufficiency, as a freehold that exempts its owner from the process of exchange. (Jefferson's reference to "the chosen people of God" suggests a meeting point between the apocalyptic and agrarian traditions. The citizen farmer is the Israelite *redivivus* of Jefferson's republican millennium.) The tradesman, artisan, or landless laborer, in contrast, is unfit for liberty because he depends on others for his livelihood and can be made to serve their interests and ambitions. Commerce and manufactures create a world governed by human whim and the fluctuations of the market; they undermine economic autonomy by replacing real property with the mobile property of exchange.

Jefferson, in sum, rests his case for a yeoman commonwealth on the different effects on society and personality of land on the one hand, and portable wealth such as commodities or paper money on the other. Although few contemporaries went so far in their hostility to the marketplace — and Jefferson himself was less doctrinaire in other pronouncements — many Americans shared his adherence to agrarianism and felt as he did that Hamilton's financial program threatened civic virtue. To George Logan of Philadelphia, who published under the pseudonym "A Farmer," it seemed evident that the measures of the government would tend to "undermine the liberties of our country." The funding of the public debt, he wrote in 1791, was an "unjust and ruinous invention" to add "to the wealth of monied men" while impoverishing virtuous yeomen. Hugh Henry Brackenridge, an ardent Jeffersonian, protested two years later that the funding acts discredited "common industry" by producing "sudden losses and sudden gains to individuals." In his novel *Modern Chivalry,* Brackenridge condemned speculation and asserted that the motto of a sound economy should be the farmer's "as ye sow, so shall ye reap."

Those who rejected the Jeffersonian or Country ideology found much to say in favor of a morality and a polity based on mobile rather than real wealth. Theorists friendly to the market commonly pointed out that agricultural life was backward and provincial; they emphasized the role of commerce in fostering culture and the mechanical arts. Far from making a virtue of self-sufficiency, such thinkers enumerated the benefits that stemmed from buying and selling. According to Montesquieu, a respected authority on republicanism both in England and America, trade cured narrow prejudices and softened barbarous manners. Indeed, *le doux commerce,* as it was called in the eighteenth century, was often praised by its defenders for building mutual confidence and teaching men to care for one another. Whereas the husbandman extolled by Jeffersonians could theoretically stand alone, relying on no one but himself, the man engaged in exchange relations was compelled to trust and depend on others in order to conduct his business. As a correspondent to the *Massachusetts Gazette* put it in 1787, "the spirit of commerce is the great bond of union among citizens." Summing up the traditional arguments for a commercial commonwealth, the writer added that trade furnished a nation's people with employment, supplied their mutual wants, and by "producing reciprocal dependencies," rendered "the whole system harmonious and energetic."

Alexander Hamilton drew upon this ideological tradition in setting forth his proposals to secure the public credit and charter a national bank. Prosperity and unity, he believed, were stronger safeguards of a people's liberty than the austere virtue of the solitary husbandman. In his reports to Congress, he insisted that a funded debt was essential to promote economic growth and "to cement more closely the union of the states." In contrast to Jefferson, who attributed so much value to ownership of land, Hamilton spoke admiringly of the intangible qualities required for commercial success, whether in nations or individuals: "confidence," "respectability," and the wearing of "a proper countenance." He saw no cause for alarm in an economic system that operated on nothing more substantial than judgment and appearance: "In nothing are appearances of greater moment, than in whatever regards credit. Opinion is the soul of it, and this is affected by appearances, as well as realities." To Jeffersonians, a republic so dependent on "caprice" would not long retain its freedom; but Hamiltonians dismissed such fears in projecting a vision of America made rich and powerful through manufacturing and trade.

The Hamiltonian-Jeffersonian dialogue persisted with certain variations into the nineteenth century, as the United States transformed itself from an agrarian to a market society, and many American writers contributed to it in their literature. Charles Brockden Brown, the first American novelist of note, pondered its implications in his most important work, *Arthur Mervyn,* which was written on the eve of Jefferson's election. Brown himself calls attention to this aspect of the novel in a critical essay on his fictional theory and practice entitled "Walstein's School of

History." Commenting on the intellectual system of an author named Engel—a thinly disguised self-portrait—he maintains that the most extensive source of relations among men "is property."

> No topic can engage the attention of man more momentous than this. Opinions, relative to property, are the immediate source of nearly all the happiness and misery that exist among mankind. If men were guided by justice in the acquisition and disbursement, the brood of private and public evils would be extinguished.

The novel proper explores the change in Arthur Mervyn's mind and character as he makes his way from the agrarian hinterland to Philadelphia, the seat of the nation's finances, its cultural life, and a yellow fever epidemic. Weighing the loss of artless virtue against the growth of sophistication and social intercourse, Brown concludes only that the commercial future is as inevitable as it seems ambiguous.

Brown also anticipates many of the central themes of the American Renaissance. The major prose writers of the antebellum period produced their greatest works in the decades following Jackson's attack on the U.S. Bank, and it is not surprising that in this intense ideological climate—so similar in some respects to the 1790s—they should have turned their attention to economic issues. Emerson's *Nature* begins with a section entitled "Commodity"; Thoreau's *Walden* opens with the chapter "Economy"; Hawthorne introduces *The Scarlet Letter* with an account of his tenure in the Salem custom house; and Melville's narrator Ishmael complains of his poverty in the second sentence of *Moby-Dick.* As such examples suggest, these authors are concerned with the impact of exchange relations on society and the individual, including the writer himself who has to please the public in order to sell his books.

Melville and Thoreau are perhaps the most outspoken in condemning the depredations of capitalism, but they arrive at such radically different conclusions as almost to recapitulate in their literature the original conflict between the Court and the Country. A profound critic of commercial civilization, Melville nevertheless accepts its inevitability and suggests that the interdependence of working men under division of labor can form the basis of a new fraternal order. In *Moby-Dick,* he uses an image drawn from trade to affirm his faith in human brotherhood: "It's a mutual, joint-stock world, in all meridians. We cannibals must help these Christians." Thoreau, on the other hand, calls for complete withdrawal from the process of exchange and celebrates an ideal of self-sufficiency for which husbandry—the cultivation of his bean field—becomes a metaphor. Much like Jefferson, he believes that the commercial spirit is incompatible with liberty, noting that the marketplace has reduced his countrymen, if not to the "tools" of demagogues, at least to desperate slave-drivers of themselves. Coming nearly seventy years after the *Notes on Virginia*, Thoreau's strictures on the "subservience and venality" of his neighbors underscore the continuance of agrarian ideology in American culture:

> It is very evident what mean and sneaking lives many of you live… seeking to curry favor, to get custom, by how many modes, only not state-prison offenses; lying, flattering, voting, contracting your-selves into a nutshell of civility, or dilating into an atmosphere of thin and vaporous generosity, that you may persuade your neigh-bor to let you make his shoes, or his hat, or his coat, or his carriage, or import his groceries for him; making yourselves sick, that you may lay up something against a sick day…no matter how much or how little.

III

Of the thirteen essays collected in this volume, four deal pri-marily with the seventeenth century. Edwin C. Rozwenc examines John Smith's vision of the New World as both "a place in which to achieve personal honor and glory" and an opportunity for men to better themselves economically. Perry Miller, the dean of Ameri-can Puritan studies, gives an analysis of the plain style and argues that the Puritans' preference for direct and unadorned expression has been their most enduring legacy to later generations. Taking a somewhat different view of Puritan aesthetics, Robert Daly emphasizes the potentiality for poetry in an attitude that found types or symbols everywhere in the sensible world. Richard Slot-kin provides still another perspective on the colonial imagination in his discussion of the captivity narrative as a parable of personal and communal "salvation-through-affliction."

Lewis P. Simpson introduces the eighteenth century with his

essay on Robert Beverley and William Byrd II, two Southern authors who attempted to incorporate slavery into the pastoral ideal. Ursula Brumm writes on Jonathan Edwards as a forerunner of the American symbolists, claiming, in contrast to Daly, that Edwards was original in applying typological method to the interpretation of nature. Benjamin Franklin is the subject of an essay by Robert F. Sayre, who offers a reading of the *Autobiography* and calls attention to Franklin's gift for trying out "provisional identities." Kenneth Silverman focuses on the Revolutionary period in his study of literary Whiggery and its meaning for the colonists. Eric Foner's essay on Thomas Paine brings out the connection between Paine's use of clear, forceful language and his anti-deferential politics (and confirms, incidentally, the accuracy of Miller's remarks about the influence of the plain style on Revolutionary rhetoric). Two essays consider the importance for early American culture of the Scottish Enlightenment. Garry Wills argues that Thomas Jefferson concluded from his reading of Francis Hutcheson that all men are equal in their possession of the moral sense. And Michael Davitt Bell analyzes the novels of Charles Brockden Brown in relation to the Scottish school's mistrust of art and the imagination.

There are, finally, two essays that consider more broadly the implications for later American literature of colonial habits of thought. Sacvan Bercovitch locates the uniqueness of the American imagination in its image of America as both self and nation—an image, he believes, that originated with the Puritans. Kenneth B. Murdock sees certain values as characteristic of American literature, most notably an emphasis on the self-made man or the farmer-pioneer. Murdock's essay seemed an appropriate choice to conclude the volume, for he finds that this particular attitude can be traced back to John Smith and his "image of America."

For helpful suggestions in preparing this anthology, I would like to express my thanks to Daniel Aaron, Everett Emerson, Alan Heimert, Keneth Kinnamon, David Levin, and Richard Strier.

Captain John Smith's Image of America

by Edwin C. Rozwenc

Nearly a hundred years ago, John Gorham Palfrey, a devoted student of New England's antiquities, remarked to Henry Adams that he had certain historic doubts as to the story of Captain John Smith and Pocahontas. An article in the *North American Review* on that subject, he suggested, "would attract as much attention, and probably break as much glass, as any other stone that could be thrown by a beginner."[1] Adams' essay on Captain John Smith in the *North American Review* was a full-scale attack on Smith's veracity as a historian. He centered his attack on the Pocahontas story as it appears in *The Generall Historie of Virginia, New England and the Summer Isles* published more than a decade after Smith had written his first brief account of his adventures in the New World. Adams frankly stated that his purpose was "nothing less than the entire erasure of one of the more attractive portions of American history."[2]

For a generation or more after Henry Adams' famous essay, Smith became the subject of one of the most celebrated controversies in American history. To a certain extent, the quarrel over

[1]Henry Adams, *The Education of Henry Adams* (New York, 1931), p. 222. Henry Adams' account of the genesis of his essay on Captain John Smith makes the episode briefer than it really was. Actually, Adams began his investigations in the British Museum in 1861 and the article in the *North American Review* was not published until 1867. See letters to Palfrey and Charles Deane in Harold Cater, *Henry Adams and His Friends* (Boston, 1947), pp. 8-23, 29-36.

[2]Henry Adams, "Captain John Smith," in *Chapters of Erie and other Essays* (Boston, 1871), p. 193. The original article appeared in the *North American Review*, CIV (Jan., 1867), 1-30.

Smith's reputation as a historian became a sectional battle in which Southern writers, particularly Virginians, sought to defend Smith against a Yankee conspiracy to defame him.[3] More recent scholarship, however, demonstrates that there is substantial truth in Smith's historical writings, even in the fantastic European adventures recorded in *The True Travels, Adventures, and Observations of Captain John Smith*.[4]

The interminable debate as to whether the dramatic Pocahontas story can be preserved as part of a true record of the American historical experience has diverted attention from other important questions about Captain John Smith. Those we raise must be concerned with more than the truthfulness of his historical accounts, important—and fascinating—as such questions may be. The redoubtable Captain's accounts of the settlement of Virginia lie athwart the starting point of our history and in one way or another we must come to terms with them. His writings, indeed, are one of the first attempts to make an imaginative reconstruction of the origins and meaning of the American experience.

Every man's vision is directed by the metaphors which rule his mind. We must, therefore, seek to discover how Captain Smith chose to give order and meaning to his experiences in the New World: what models of historical reporting were available to him and what resources could he draw upon out of the imaginative experience of Europeans to construct his own narrative? In the light of these questions, we begin to see how a spirit of knight-errantry and the yearnings of a self-made man are interwoven in his conception of America and its possibilities.

The Generall Historie, which contains the fullest account of Smith's experiences in America, adds new dimensions to the

[3]See Jarvis M. Morse, "John Smith and His Critics...," *Journal of Southern History,* I (1935), 124. Edward Channing was certain that the controversy was used "to stimulate Southern hatred of New England scholars." *A History of the United States,* I (New York, 1905), 174.

[4]See Bradford Smith, *Captain John Smith: His Life and Legend* (Philadelphia, New York, 1953). The author attempts a full-scale defense of the truth of the *True Travels* as well as Smith's other historical writings. See Chap. 2 and especially appended essay by Laura Polanyi Striker, pp. 311-342. See also Philip L. Barbour, "Captain John Smith's Route through Turkey and Russia," *William and Mary Quarterly,* 3d Ser., XIV (July 1957), 358-369, and prefatory essay by Laura Polanyi Striker in the new edition of Henry Wharton's *The Life of John Smith, English Soldier* (Chapel Hill, 1957), pp. 1-31.

literary conventions of the chivalric romance. The third and fourth books, particularly, have a dramatic rhythm and an exciting vividness that charmed Americans for generations until Henry Adams began to throw his stones. Excitement and suspense are at high pitch throughout the *Generall Historie;* surprise attacks and ambuscades, spectacular Indian fights in boats and canoes as well as in the forest, colorful Indian feasts, dances and ceremonies fill its pages. The creation of tension prior to the deliverance by Pocahontas is a little masterpiece of dramatic preparation. Our hero is tied to a tree, and Indian braves dance around him, painted in a fearful manner, shaking rattles and shouting; there are orations, with the chief priest speaking in a "hellish voyce," and the pitting of white man's magic against Indian magic. Throughout the narrative, Captain Smith looms above all other men, matching wits with a wily and resourceful Powhatan, issuing commands, performing acts of individual heroism when personal bravery was the last resource.[5]

The *General Historie,* indeed, breathes a spirit that we associate with the popular romances of the Elizabethan Age. As Smith grew to manhood on a Lincolnshire farm, the vogue of the medieval chivalric romance was at its height in England. Popular versions of the knightly deeds of Guy of Warwick, Tom of Lincoln, and Palmerin of England fell from the presses like autumn leaves and fed the imaginations of middle-class readers for generations.

Although little is known of Smith's reading habits, Bradford Smith has reminded us that the Captain's imagination was fired by the heroic models of the knightly romance.[6] In the autobiographical *True Travels,* written a few years after the *Generall Historie,* Smith chooses to recall that, when a young man, he left his home for a time and retired to a wooded area. "Here by a faire brook he built a Pavillon of boughes, where only in his cloaths he lay. His study was *Machiavills* Art of warre and *Marcus Aurelius;* his exercise a good horse, with his lance and Ring; his food was thought to be more of venison than anything else. ..." His life as a knightly hermit attracted notice and he was soon in-

[5]*Travels and Works of Captain John Smith,* ed. Edward Arber (Edinburgh, 1910), II, 395-400. Hereafter cited as Smith, *Works.*
[6]Bradford Smith, *Captain John Smith,* pp. 26-27, 36-39.

vited to Tattersall Castle, the seat of Henry, Earl of Lincoln, where he was taught the finer arts of horsemanship by an Italian riding master. Afterwards, he went to the Low Countries to begin his series of "brave adventures" across Europe.[7]

The romantic hermitage in the forest by "a faire brook" smacks of a Robin Hood without followers. There are resemblances, too, to certain familiar patterns in the Arthurian romances. Tom of Lincoln and Bevis of Hampton lived in fields and forests as shepherd boys until their true nobility could be put to the test before the princes and ladies of the world.

As for Smith's later adventures in Europe, we are reminded of Guy of Warwick who "enjoyed" his ladylove to watch and wait while he proved himself by "deeds." He then set sail for Normandy and fought his way through Flanders, Spain, and Lombardy, eventually to fight the Saracens at Constantinople. Smith followed a similar pattern of great deeds from the Low Countries across Europe to the Hungarian plains. There, in single combats before the eyes of the two armies, "the Rampiers all beset with fair Dames," Smith slew three Turkish champions with lance, pistol, and battle-ax. Their decapitated heads were mounted on lances at the subsequent ceremony, and the General of the army bestowed on Smith a promotion, "a faire Horse richly furnished," and a "Semitere and belt worth three hundred ducats."[8]

Like many a knight of old, Smith was rescued by a fair lady at the moment of direst peril—not once, but three times. The beauteous Lady Tragabigzanda aided him when he was a captive of the Turks; the Lady Callamata gave him succor after he arrived half dead from his fearful flight from Turkish captivity across the Russian steppes to the Don; and Pocahontas saved his life in the New World whence he had gone to add new deeds to the brave adventures already accomplished in the Old. Unlike the heroes of knightly romances however, Smith never had affairs of love with his rescuers. They were stage deities who intervened at the proper moments, and always women of high rank—an aid no doubt to Smith's pretensions to being a gentleman, coat of arms and all.

The fantastic adventures recorded in the *True Travels* were regarded by Henry Adams as partly fictitious and as a further

[7]Smith, *Works,* II, 823.
[8]*Ibid.,* 838-840.

reason for impugning the reliability of Smith's writings. More recent investigations have shown us that the inconsistencies and seeming inventions in Smith's writings are greatly outnumbered by reports and observations that have successfully passed the critical scrutiny of geographers, anthropologists, and historians. Henry Adams' generation was enthralled by the possibilities of scientific history, and Adams himself sought to discover whether history could be written "by the severest process of stating, with the least possible comment, such facts as seemed sure." Nevertheless the artist and the scientist are as inseparably connected in all of his historical writing as the two opposite faces of an ancient deity. Perhaps if Henry Adams had not been a mere "beginner" when he wrote his essay on Captain John Smith, he might have been able to appreciate that Smith's historical writing was affected by the popular literary attitudes of Elizabethan and Jacobean England.

Yet the influence of popular literary taste alone cannot account for the character of Smith's historical writing. We must remember also that the conceptions of the nature of history and of the office of the historian as it was held in Smith's day differ greatly from our own. When Smith's *Generall Historie* was written, one of the most widely read historians in England was Sir Walter Raleigh. In a panegyric on history prefixed to his own *History of the World,* Raleigh wrote:

> True it is, that among other benefits, for which History hath been honoured, in this one it triumpheth over all human knowledge—that it hath given us life in our understanding, Since the world itself and life and beginning, even to this day: yea it hath triumphed over time, which besides it, nothing but eternity hath triumphed over. ... And it is not the least debt we owe to History, that it hath made us acquainted with our dead ancestors and out of the depth and darkness of the earth, delivered us of their memory and fame.

The end and scope of history, Raleigh wrote, was to "teach by example of times past such wisdom as may guide our desires and actions"; the memory and the fame of the great deeds of men were the best examples.[9]

[9]See Charles H. Firth's "Sir Walter Raleigh's History of the World," *Proceeding of the British Academy,* 1917-18, pp. 427-446. Quotations taken from pp. 432-433.

No less was Captain John Smith a child of the Elizabethan Age. In 1630, he wrote, "Seeing honour is our lives ambition, and our ambition after death, to have an honourable memory of our life: and seeing by no meanes we would be abated of the dignitie and glory of our predecessors, let us imitate their vertues to be worthily their successors. ..."[10] His opening lines in the third book of the *Generall Historie,* which relates the dramatic story of the founding of Virginia, express his desire for the "eternizing of the memory of those that effected it."[11]

Smith's concept of history and his literary imagination gave him the proper dress with which to clothe his image of America. The deeds of Englishmen in Virginia were as worthy of being eternized as those of the Spaniards in Peru and Mexico. Although no gold and silver were discovered in Virginia, Smith saw much that was wondrous in the accomplishments of "those that the three first yeares began this Plantation; notwithstanding all their factions, mutinies, and miseries, so gently corrected, and well prevented. ..." He challenged his readers to "peruse the *Spanish Decades,* the Relations of Master *Hackluit,* and tell me how many ever with such small meanes as a Barge of 22 *(or rather two)* tuns, sometimes with seaven, eight, or nine, or but at most, twelve or sixteene men, did ever so discover so many fayre and navigable Rivers, subject so many severall Kings, people, and Nations, to obedience and contribution, with so little bloudshed."[12]

We can understand, therefore, why so much is related about Smith's explorations and Indian fights, and so little is told us of the day-by-day events at Jamestown. Whatever his motives to puff up his personal reputation, history was a matter of the glories and great deeds of men—not their prosaic daily affairs.

Yet we must not be led into a mistaken idea of John Smith's conception of America by the romantic glitter of many of the narrative passages in the *Generall Historie.* America was not simply another field of action for a bold knight. America was a land of opportunity—where men of enterprise might create a flourishing social order. The idea of America that is revealed in other portions of Smith's writing is filled with expectations of great op-

[10]Smith, *Works,* II, 936.
[11]*Ibid.,* 385.
[12]*Ibid.,* 465.

portunity for the individual even if the society of the New World does not change all of the distinctions of the English social order. John Smith was a self-made gentleman and the impulses that made for social mobility in Elizabethan England are writ large in his estimate of the New World's possibilities.

In the sixth book of the *Generall Historie* dealing with the prospects of New England, Smith asks:

> Who can desire more content that hath small meanes, or but onely his merit to advance his fortunes, than to tread and plant that ground he hath purchased by the hazard of his life; if hee have but the taste of vertue and magnanimity, what to such a minde can bee more pleasant than planting and building a foundation for his posterity, got from rude earth by Gods blessing and his owne industry without prejudice to any....

America is not primarily a place for the soldier-knight; it beckons to the industrious who are willing to build a fortune for themselves and their posterity. But America offers more than a good chance for fortune hunters; it presents the opportunity for creating a happier and more enlightened society. In the same passage, he asks further:

> What so truly sutes with honour and honesty, as the discovering things unknowne, erecting Townes, peopling Countries, informing the ignorant, reforming things unjust, teaching vertue...finde imploiment for those that are idle, because they know not what to doe: so farre from wronging any, as to cause posterity to remember thee; and remembering thee, ever honour that remembrance with praise.[13]

This is a magnificent dream of America's possibilities, one which drew thousands of Englishmen to America's shores and is still with us in many respects. But we must remember that this vision of social opportunity is not one of a society of yeoman farmers each relatively equal to the other in his station in life. Much has been made of Captain Smith's effort to organize the labor of the Jamestown settlers when he was president by laying down the rule that "he that will not worke, shall not eate." Yet we must not assume that he was responding to the wilderness environment by instituting a rough-and-ready frontier equal-

[13]*Ibid.*, 722-723.

itarianism. This was the order of a military captain seeking to maintain discipline, not that of a social visionary seeking to create a new social order in which manual labor was to have the highest value. Elsewhere, when Smith recounts the story of how he made "two gallants...both proper Gentlemen" cut down trees till their tender fingers were blistered, he hastens to add: "By this, let no man thinke that the President, and these Gentlemen spent their times as common Woodhaggers at felling of trees, or such other like labours; or that they were pressed to it as hirelings, or common slaves; for what they did, after they were but once a little inured, it seemed, and some conceited it, onely as a pleasure and recreation."[14] Smith was too proud of his coat of arms acquired by valorous exploits in Transylvania to war upon a social system based on honor and distinction.

Nevertheless, something in Captain Smith, perhaps the hard core of common sense of a man who makes his own way, made him realize that the destiny of North America would not lie with gold and silver treasure. One cause of his quarrels with other leaders in Jamestown had been his opposition to vain searches after fool's gold; he preferred to direct the energies of the men at Jamestown into hacking trees, cutting clapboards, and making pitch and potash for shipment to England. Smith's vision of America is closer to that of Richard Hakluyt and Sir Humphrey Gilbert who thought of America as a place where a balanced English society would grow, producing commodities of use to the mother country and serving as a market for the profit of English merchants and manufacturers.[15]

America was more than a land of profit and contentment, even more than a land of honor and virtue; it was a presence of great natural beauty. A tireless explorer and map-maker whose observations in Virginia and New England contributed much to the geographical knowledge of the time, Smith was also a man who felt the power and the charm of Nature in the New World. Often his descriptions have the obvious purpose of advertising the New World to prospective immigrants—the climate is tem-

[14]*Ibid.*, 439.
[15]*Cf.* George B. Parks, *Richard Hakluyt and the English Voyages* (New York, 1928), pp. 89-98; also David B. Quinn, *Raleigh and the British Empire* (New York, 1949), pp. 16-17.

perate, the soil fertile, the woods abound with wild fruits and game, the waters swim with fish in plenty—but there are also frequent flashes of subjective responses to "glistering tinctures" of water rushing over the rocks in a mountain stream, "sweet brookes and christall springs," the awesome, craggy "clifty rocks" of the Maine coast near Penobscot, the "high sandy clifts" and "large long ledges" along the coast of Massachusetts Bay. By 1616, Smith had become a convinced "northern man" among those in England who were seeking to promote other colonial ventures in America. He speaks of Massachusetts as the "Paradice of all those parts" and declares "of all the foure parts of the world that I have yet seene not inhabited...I would rather live here than any where."[16] To be sure, any honest New Englander will grant that Smith often exaggerates the fertility of the soil in New England and the moderateness of the climate, but no one can doubt that the natural beauty of the land had cast a spell on the Captain that exceeded the requirements of seventeenth-century advertising!

Aside from short voyages made to New England, Smith's experience with America was limited to the two years he lived in Virginia; yet to the end of his days his heart and mind were bewitched by America, as it was and as he dreamed it; and Americans in turn have been betwitched by him ever since. In the words of the poet:

> He is one of the first Americans we know,
> And we can claim him, though not by bond of birth,
> For we've always bred chimeras.[17]

In a very compelling sense, John Smith is an American historian—one who tried to express the meaning of events in the origins of American experience. By the modern canons of history, a man who writes of events in which he is a participant is already suspect, but, when he does so with zestful attention to his personal exploits, we are tempted to dismiss him as a braggart and a liar. Nevertheless, there is an intractable worth in John Smith's historical writings that will not allow us to cast them aside. Wesley Frank Craven says of him: "Allowing for the exaggeration of his

[16]Smith, *Works,* II, 719, I, 193-194.
[17]Stephen Vincent Benet, *Western Star* (New York, 1943), p. 72.

own importance, it must be recognized that his works contain much reliable information and that he himself was a man of real courage and strength.... His judgment of the conditions of the colony and their causes in the maladministration of the company through the years immediately preceding its fall are supported in the main by a careful study of the sources now at hand."[18]

By and large, the discrepancies of fact in his historical writing, involving as they often do such questions as the numbers of Indians who guarded him or the quantities of food served to him, are really trivial matters—the peccadillos of an amateur historian over which we need not blush any more than we do for the peccadillos of a historian of any age. The greater amount of data in Smith's historical writings has survived tests of credibility in every generation since they were published. The Pocahontas story may be an invention of Smith's mind, or of many minds in the taverns of seventeenth-century London, but on the basis of recent reexaminations of the evidence, the critical historian can admit the likelihood of Smith's deliverance by "the Indian princess" with fewer doubts than he might have had a generation ago.[19]

Smith's historical imagination is one key to our understanding of the approach of Englishmen to the New World. He wrote of a brief moment only in the minuscule beginnings of Anglo-Saxon culture in North America. But he brought to his relation of events in Virginia the spirit of knight-errantry which still had a hold upon the imaginations of men in Elizabethan and Jacobean England and gave to Englishmen a vision of America as a place in which to achieve personal honor and glory. When we remember W. J. Cash's penetrating analysis of the aristocratic ideals of the South, we can understand readily that the chivalric spirit of the *Generall Historie* makes the defense of John Smith's reputation by southerners something of an automatic reflex. The *Generall Historie* points to social attitudes and styles of life that actually became fundamental social traits in Virginia and much of the South.

[18]Wesley Frank Craven, *Dissolution of the Virginia Company* (New York, 1932), p. 5.

[19]The best recent examination of the literary legend of Pocahontas is Jay B. Hubbell's "The Smith-Pocahontas Story in Literature," *Virginia Magazine of History and Biography,* LXV (July 1957), 275-300.

But Captain John Smith is more than a totem in the Southern tradition of chivalry. After his brief trials and encounters in Virginia, he understood well that America was destiny and possibility —that America's history lay in the future. He saw that destiny in terms of opportunity for improvement. America would be a place where men might find economic betterment, not by plunderings of gold and other treasure, but in a balanced society of husbandmen, tradesmen, and merchants. The New World, withal, would be a place where men might teach virtue and establish a morality free of the encumbrances of the old. John Smith's *Generall Historie* is an important part of the deeper cultural consciousness which has sustained this perennial faith in the promise of American life.

A Colonial Dialect

by Perry Miller

In the course of the last century, or indeed of the last two centuries, within the confines of American discourse, the word "Puritan" has taken on a wholly American connotation. When, for instance, in 1826 John Randolph of Roanoke denounced the combination between John Quincy Adams and Henry Clay which, the previous year, had made Adams President, as a conspiracy of "the Puritan and the blackleg," he was not associating Adams with the majestic figures of Milton and Cromwell. He was stigmatizing Adams by an adjective that had already become in many quarters of the country, especially among Southern gentlemen, synonymous with hypocritical self-righteousness, moral snobbery, and the peddling of wooden nutmegs.

In much of literary discussion, especially since the heyday of H. L. Mencken, the term has generally been used pejoratively to mean those Americans who are afraid of life, who would impose moralistic restraints on free expression, who for long enforced the sway of the "genteel" over both creation and criticism, and who have at last been put utterly to rout by the upsurge of a vigorous, liberal, outspoken literature. Even sympathetic attempts to find meanings for our age in such "Puritanical" writers as Nathaniel Hawthorne and Emily Dickinson, or in the Puritan strains of Melville and Mark Twain, are apt to treat Puritanism as a thing of wholly native growth. They assume that it sprang full-grown from the soil of New England with the first planters of Plymouth and Massachusetts Bay, that having thus become rooted in America it has grown like some insidious poison ivy from whose roots stifling tendrils have coiled around the American soul.

It is perhaps useless to protest that originally the name "Puritan" was applied to those who wanted to purify the institution established by the Elizabethan Settlement in the Church of England of the remnants of medieval ritual and polity. It is still more idle to insist that these English Puritans were not a peculiar English sect but that they were members of an international movement which is best subsumed under the term "Calvinist." English Puritanism no doubt took on distinctive characteristics because of the special situation in England, but essentially it was at one with the Protestantism of the Continent—that Protestantism which could not rest with what it considered the halfway measures of Lutheranism or Anglicanism. In contemporary Britain, whether in the *Times Literary Supplement* or over the BBC, the word "Puritanism" is seldom or never used with the same implications as in America. Several surrogates have taken over—most notably "the Nonconformist conscience" or "evangelicalism"— which indicate how, in English society, Puritanism after 1660 diffused itself into a frame of mind rather than remaining an ecclesiastical program. For the English, "Puritanism" signifies that historical party which rose in rebellion against Charles I, reached its crest of power under Cromwell, disintegrated during the Restoration, and dissolved under the Act of Toleration. It has little modern relevance, except as its descendants have retained a few vestigial traits.

Insofar as a religious motivation propelled Englishmen to emigrate to New England, that impulse was not theological but ecclesiastical. The colony intended first of all to set up a New Testament polity, to follow the New Testament prescription of how a pure church should be instituted, and to the realization of this true Christian polity, all other purposes, political and social, were to be subordinated. Hence the major literary productions of the first generation in New England are treatises on polity— those of Cotton, Davenport, Richard Mather, Norton, and above all Thomas Hooker's *Survey of the Summe of Church-Discipline*. It was only as events in England—the ironic developments of the

Civil Wars, or the utterly unpredicted workings-out of strife on the Continent, where concrete programs of church polity had to be relegated to matters indifferent—left the New Englanders with no countries to convert except their own, that this literature eventually became the badge of a colonial eccentricity.

In England, for the whole complex of bibliolatry, Nonconformism, evangelicalism, Matthew Arnold in 1869 coined the term "Hebraism," which, he declared in *Culture and Anarchy,* inculcates "strictness of conscience" as against "spontaneity of consciousness," and to "the book which contains this invaluable law they call the Word of God" attributes "a reach and sufficiency coextensive with all the wants of human nature." I do not know whether in 1869 English Nonconformists to any sizable degree accepted Arnold's charge that they took the Bible as adequate to meeting all the wants of human nature, but in America the heritage of colonial Puritanism worked in a quite different setting. Historians are still not clear just how far the Great Migration of 1630 really intended to go toward setting up a pure "Bible Commonwealth." When codification of the first statutes became imperative, John Cotton drew up a digest in 1641, usually known as "Moses His Judicials." It is about as close to literal Biblicism as one can come, but already there were forces in the tiny community that could not stomach it; so Nathaniel Ward, who had studied the common law as well as divinity, framed the "Body of Liberties," which the General Court did officially adopt and which, severe though it may seem by our standards, is as much indebted to secular precedents as to the Old Testament. Furthermore, the fact of the matter was that all the while these Puritans were staking their lives and fortunes on a vindication of the authentic church polity, they were also deeply implicated in the Parliamentary struggle against the Stuarts.

I have elsewhere tried to describe the vast concourse of ideas and systems of thought the Puritans brought with them into the wilderness which in actuality was derived not, as they supposed their polity was, by direct deduction from the Bible but from the contemporaneous world of the intellect. They carried with them not only the Bible itself but that elaborate superstructure which we call Calvinism and which for them found ultimate formulation in the *Westminster Confession.* Above all, they brought with them an organon of logic which they assumed was so simple and obvious as to be beyond question, and which they serenely employed for the exposition of sacred texts without the slightest awareness that the results which men extract from these texts vary inversely to the squares of the number of methods used in interpretation. Without the slightest suspicion that they were doing anything but taking at face value the words of the Bible, they translated these into the terminology of a complex psychological conception—that of the "faculties"—which had come down to them not from Hebrew sources but from Aristotle and scholasticism, and which, even as they were perfecting their expositions, was already shattered by Descartes and would soon be interred by John Locke. Here again we can see what the process of colonization means: in the realm of matter, it requires subduing a wilderness to towns and agriculture; in the realm of the mind it leads to being subdued by the emptiness of explicit victory, with the consequent necessity, which can be extremely painful, of having to construct a coherence out of implicit assumptions.

As the core of bibliolatry shrank, particularly as the argument for a strict application of New Testament polity became irrelevant, even meaningless, the Puritan intellect was reduced to digging for clues as to its meaning among the shards and remnants of what had originally been these vast, majestic assumptions. And because in the general debacle of strict Biblicism it also lost its apparatus of logical discourse—the dialectic of both Aristotle and Ramus could not long survive Descartes and Locke—and by the same token saw the dissolution of its doctrines of the human faculties, American Puritanism had in fact only one tool left with which to explore the secret caverns of its soul. But Puritanism still possessed the trusty spade with which it had from the beginning dug its foundations: the word. Though the universe might change from Ptolemaic to Copernican, and from an intricate machinery of faculties into a Lockean creature of pure sensation, the word would still serve this culture, because it had always seen the word as primarily a serviceable thing. In Europe and in England life was so complicated that even Calvinists learned to speak and write with baroque flourishes. But this society, thanks to its colonial isolation, which for so long has seemed an affliction, could now perceive the hand of providence. The founders had dedicated it irrevocably to what they called the "plain style." Through thick and thin, through wars, plagues, revolutions, they had never, or seldom, yielded to the temptation to use the word to ornament their woes. If their dialect had to be provincial, very well, but let it be their own: let it be defiantly plain!

This term, "the plain style," is not something that I have devised or that some ingenious historian has invented, like "metaphysical," "Augustan," or "Victorian," as a convenience in narration. It was consciously used by the Puritans themselves. In their minds it was a shorthand expression for a vast body of rhetorical, psychological, and theological conviction, all of which centered on a doctrine of how the word, spoken or written, should properly be managed. For instance: during several years John Cotton was renowned as one of the most eloquent preachers at the University of Cambridge; crowds came to revel in his erudition and fancy, much as other crowds came to admire the spectacle of John Donne at St. Paul's in London. But John Cotton underwent a conversion; he became a Puritan. He advertised this event not by announcing a change of opinion but simply by abruptly, on a particular Sabbath, commencing to speak in the plain style. He had uttered no more than five sentences before his auditors knew what had happened. The difference between "the *mode* of the University" and the Puritan mode was so striking that it was almost as though he had suddenly started to speak in another language. The founders of New England thus brought to these shores not only a highly developed theology, cosmology, logic, psychology, and a sophisticated concept of state and society: they also brought a doctrine of the word. Because they utilized this doctrine to make themselves understood both in their congregations and ceremonial observations, and in their publications, either through the presses of London or else, later, through their crude presses in Cambridge and Boston, they bequeathed their principles to America.

To be sure, Puritan writers were not irrevocably bound to employ it on all occasions. Nathaniel Ward deliberately shoved it aside for *The Simple Cobler of Aggawam in America,* of 1647; Captain Edward Johnson tried to cultivate a more ornate manner in telling of *The Wonder-Working Providence of Sions Saviour* in 1654; Cotton Mather risked and almost achieved bathos by casting his *Magnalia Christi Americana* of 1702 in a curiously hysterical prose which, however it may be characterized, is assuredly not "plain"; while Edward Taylor, as we have only recently become aware, struggled in the solitude of his study in frontier Westfield to subdue the sensuous impulses of a "metaphysical" technique to the rigorous impositions of his creed.

However, the existence of these sports amid the orthodox utterances merely serves to reinforce the moral that on occasions where the Puritan position most required exposition—which is to say, in the sermon, the treatise on polity, the history, the explanation of political theory—the Puritan spokesman picked up the plain style as readily as he picked up a hoe instead of an axe. Governor William Bradford, who had lived through the grim drama of Plymouth, instinctively and surely recounted it according to the canons of simplicity, and if one wants to comprehend most immediately what the concept of the plain style meant to Puritans, he has only to read any paragraph of Bradford's *History of Plimouth Plantation.*

One may select almost at random. For an example of the plain style at its finest, there is Bradford's account of what the separatist exiles confronted once they had escaped from England and were striving to hold their community together in Leyden, in Holland:

> Being now come into the Low Countries, they saw many goodly and fortified cities, strongly walled and guarded with troops of armed men. Also, they heard a strange and uncouth language, and beheld the different manners and customs of the people, with their strange fashions and attires; all so far differing from that of their plain country villages (wherein they were bred and had so long lived) as it seemed they were come into a new world. But these were not the things they much looked on, or long took up their thoughts, for they had other work in hand and another kind of war to wage and maintain. For although they saw fair and beautiful cities, flowing with abundance of all sorts of wealth and riches, yet it was not long before they saw the grim and grisly face of poverty coming upon them like an armed man, with whom they must buckle and encounter, and from whom they could not fly. But they were armed with faith and patience against him and all his encounters; and though they were sometimes foiled, yet by God's assistance, they prevailed and got the victory.

Note the haunting couplings, nearly yet never quite becoming redundant, so obvious, so generalized that they seem at first sight to tell little about the situation, but which upon second reading tell everything about exile and forlornness: "goodly and fortified," "walled and guarded," "strange and uncouth," "wage and maintain," "grim and grisly," "buckle and encounter." What saves Bradford's prose from tedium is the way in which this device is used to restrain the passion. The very abstractness of the couplings holds experience at arm's length, thus insuring that the real point is not lost in the glitter and rush of sensation. The rhetoric folds back upon the substantive purpose; out of these pairs comes the didactic proposition, not mechanically affixed but inherently rising from the analyzed experience of the faith and patience which, with divine assistance, do prevail and gain the victory.

Puritan writings are full of theoretical expositions of the plain style, and it may be worth our while to note one or two of these theoretical statements. Thomas Hooker composed his *Survey of the Summe of Church-Discipline* just at the moment when, by accounts arriving from London, the argument between Presbyterians and Independents had come to such a dire pass that the polity vindicated, as the colonists believed, in New England seemed on the point of becoming a mere colonial experiment rather than what the founders had gloriously intended, a model for the fulfillment of English reformation. Hooker was a man who, a panegyrist said, could put a king in his pocket, but when he sent the manuscript of this work to London (where it was printed in 1648), he was already bewildered. What was happening there made no sense to him: his fellow-Congregationalists in England, now known as "Independents," were not only resisting Presbyterianism—which he could understand—but were seeking allies among heretics whom they should have despised, the enthusiastical Anabaptists and Antinomians, glossing over their apostasy with a newfangled notion of religious liberty. Hooker would have none of this: he offered a philosophy of Biblical polity within the rubrics of the old Puritan logic, but especially within the framework of solid Puritan rhetoric.

The *Survey* is a technical treatise on the polity, but what Hooker announced in his preface may also stand as the canon of composition he followed in his sermons; it provides a perfect summation of the ideal of the plain style as it was brought to New England and there made the presiding rule of American prose:

> As it is beyond my skill, so I professe it is beyond my care to please the niceness of mens palates, with any quaintnesse of language. They who covet more sauce then meat, they must provide cooks to their minds, It was a cavill cast upon Heirom, that in his writings he was *Ciceronianus non Christianus:* My rudeness frees me wholly from this exception, for being *Logos Idiotes* [ignorant of the Word], as the Apostle hath it, if I would, I could not lavish out in looseness of language, and as the case stands, if I could answer any mans desire in that daintinesse of speech, I would not do the matter that Injury which is now under my hand: *Ornari res ipsa negat.* The substance and solidity of the frame is that, which pleaseth the builder, its the painters work to provide varnish.

Ornari res ipsa negat—"the thing itself refuses to be ornamented"! There in a nutshell is the principle by which the Puritan word, the spoken or written word, must be regulated. Or as the compilers of *The Bay Psalm Book* strikingly phrased it in their preface of 1639: "If therefore the verses are not always so smooth and elegant as some may desire or expect; let them consider that Gods Altar needs not our pollishings." For the "Altar" of God was in the Puritan view not only verses in the Bible but the propositions of theology and polity, the factual record of divine providences in biographies and histories, or of the natural environment about them, the vast sea and the terrible forest. These were things in themselves; to ornament the handiwork of the Almighty was a presumption of inherent depravity: it was to set daintiness, looseness of language, above the objective facts of creation. Occasionally even Puritan writers might try to enjoy a holiday from such rigorous objectivity, and indulge themselves in a thin varnish of wit; the great ones, and even the lesser ones when dealing with the great themes, submitted themselves to the inexorable rule of substance and solidity.

This is not the place to attempt a defense of the Puritan aesthetic. Many in our age may see in Hooker's contemptuous relegation of the painter to mere provider of varnish an illustration of aesthetic starvation. In our own time there has arisen a new interest in the prose and poetry contemporaneous with Hooker and Cotton which these worthies condemned as frivolous niceness—the richly tessellated discourse of Donne, Launcelot Andrewes, and the Laudian clergy, and the densely intellectualized poetry of those we lump together as "metaphysicals." I am sure that anyone at all sensitive to the nuances of religious expression may, from time to time, even though he admires Bradford's simple majesty, cry out for the richer vocabulary and the more intricate patterns of the Anglican mode, just as one may pardonably grow weary of a steady diet of Bach and in revolt turn to Berlioz. In such moods we are not reconciled by the assurance that the Puritan plain style was far from being a crude style, that it was the result of a lengthy training in formal rhetoric, that it was a highly conscious art in which the supreme virtue was to conceal the art. The Puritan writers, within the limits determined by their creed, took pride in writing well and pleasure in their achievements. There is an excitement in the passage quoted from Bradford which, once the nature of the enterprise is appreciated, becomes quite as communicable to us as the beauty of any periods of John Donne. But the argument over whether the Puritans did or did not experience aesthetic delight in words or in nature is a stale one; fortunately we are not obliged, as they were, to embrace the one standard and repudiate the other. What at this juncture we are concerned to note is that for better or worse the Puritans did bring a completely rationalized theory of the plain style to America, and because they wrote and published so much, and because their descendants carried on their instruction, we must realize how they fastened it upon the literary conscience of America so securely that virtually all our writers, even though they come from Mississippi rather than from Connecticut, or were brought up as Catholics rather than as Puritans, have had to contend with its consequences.

To the extent that this generalization is even partially true, then there are two further aspects of the Puritan cultivation of their art which we should briefly note. Here again Thomas Hooker's preface goes straight to the point. The nature of this particular volume required him to use logical and scholastical terms, such as he would not employ in the pulpit. Even so, he was not addressing his treatise exclusively to the learned; however technical the material, it was of vital concern to all Christians, no matter how simple. Wherefore Hooker voices what is always a primary consideration in the plain style: it must address the vulgar.

> Plainesse and perspicuity, both for matter and manner of expression, are the things, that I conscientiously indeavoured in the whole debate: for I have ever thought writings that come abroad, they are not to dazzle, but direct the apprehensions of the meanest, and I have accounted the chiefest part of Iudicious learning, to make a hard point easy and familiar in explication.

We have learned to be cautious, as often pietistic celebrants of the nineteenth century were not, about hailing the Puritan founders as in any purposive sense contributing to the development of American democracy. The first Congregationalists did not consider democracy a virtue; they rejected every charge that they were in the slightest measure inclined toward egalitarianism. Still, in their concept of the uses of the word there was a democratic implication more pregnant for the future than in their idea of the covenanted church: the word in the mouth of the learned must be addressed to the "capacity of the common Auditory," to use Increase Mather's phrase. The aim of the learned was not social, it was religious; they had the tremendous responsibility of making "an ignorant man understand these Mysteries in some good measure." What they could not foresee was that eventually, after they had drilled this thought into the philosophy of American education, the rule of comprehensibility to the common man would continue to weigh upon the American writer long after he had ceased to be a preacher of theological mysteries.

Second, let me cite Hooker again to give us one of the first hints in our literature of a boast which was steadily to resound through later writings. The ideal of plainness in style was, of course, formulated among European Protestants, and Hooker needed to say no more in his preface than that he was obeying the precepts of the same academic masters which both they and he had studied; however, he began his passage with an apology which would strike them as astonishingly novel:

> That the discourse comes forth in such a homely dresse and course habit, the Reader must be desired to consider, It comes *out of the*

> *wildernesse,* where curiosity is not studied. Planters if they can pro-
> vide cloth to go warm, they leave the cutts and lace to those that
> study to go fine.

Hereafter, we have an augmenting iteration of this plea, through
the prose of Benjamin Franklin, through the cultivated rusticities
of the epistles of several Revolutionary "farmers," into the very
language of the Declaration of Independence. We are plain
speakers not so much because we learned simplicity in European
universities, but because we have to do with the wilderness. It
was, let me repeat, no part of the original Puritan conception
that ministers should make eschatological conundrums clear to
the common auditory because those peoples dwelt in a savage
land. Puritan divines were to speak to yeomen in Lancashire, to
shepherds in Northumberland, yet also to such gentry as Winthrop and Bradstreet. But out of New England first arose, and
subsequently grew, the argument that an immigrant stock no
longer had time to heed "cutts and laces." In a wilderness setting,
the plain style, without changing a single syllable of its formal
profession, subtly, rapidly became no longer a manifesto of the
scholars but a method of dealing with the environment.

The mere fact that Thomas Hooker, in so elaborately "scho-
lastic" a work as the *Survey,* smuggled this plea into his preface
is an eloquent confession of how even the first generation,
educated in England and Holland, were already losing contact
with the great world they had virtually rejected, though they
had never intended the rejection. Their sons, their grandsons,
those who never knew Cambridge, Leyden, Strasbourg, unless by
report, would find themselves insisting upon a hearing not because they wrote a Protestant rhetoric but because they were
Protestants in the wilderness. In this development, one fact stands
out: in rhetoric the *result* of a once highly elaborated doctrine
could survive, could prove its utility. In virtually every other
department of thought and expression, the original assumptions,
the machinery of proof, fell away and can hardly be recovered
by modern research. The ancient cosmology yielded to the
triumph of Newton; patterns of logic were replaced by those of
eighteenth-century speech. Even in the vital business of political
theory, Governor Winthrop's expositions of the social compact in
1645 had become archaic language by 1745 and were utterly ig-

nored in the patriotic sermons of 1776. Indeed, by the time the plain style becomes the instrument, the wonderfully effective instrument, for stating a Revolutionary case against the government of George III, hardly any practitioner of the method has the slightest memory of Petrus Ramus, of Omer Talon, or of the host who instructed the first Puritans. The intellectual revolution of the seventeenth century—in cosmology, logic, psychology—had in effect obliterated the philosophical premises of the Puritan migration. In all these areas, inhabitants of an American wilderness had been obliged, bit by bit, to make their adjustments. But in one respect they did not need to change: they might forget the rhetorical methods inculcated at early Harvard, but when the task descended upon them of speaking out, plainly and as citizens of the wilderness, they had no problem about finding a mode of utterance. The consequence of their seventeenth-century discipline remained with them long after the tuition had faded, and in the language of Revolutionary ardor, determined to speak to the common auditory and glorying in their rusticity, spokesmen of the Revolution conveyed the plain style into the extending vistas of American self-expression.

Puritan Poetics

by Robert Daly

Living in a symbolic world, the Puritans found types, or symbols, in both their Bible and their own experiences. Samuel Mather had argued that man could not *make* types: "It is not safe to make any thing a Type merely upon our own fancies and imaginations; it is God's Prerogative to make *Types.*"[1] But no commandment forbade man to *see* types, and Puritans saw them everywhere. Though Perry Miller and Ursula Brumm have asserted that Edwards was original in extending the typological method from Biblical exegesis to a reading of the spiritual significances of the sensible world, it is clear that this method had been practiced by medieval writers and by the Puritans of the seventeenth century. They, like Edwards after them, saw "the natural world (the only one accessible to human comprehension)" as "the image of and the key to the transcendent world of religion, which could thus be understood indirectly." Like him, and like their medieval predecessors, they believed that "the things of the world are ordered [and] designed to shadow forth spiritual things." They, like Edward Taylor, saw "the world slickt up in types."[2]

[1]Samuel Mather, *The Figures or Types of the Old Testament* (1683), 2nd ed. (1705; rpt. New York, 1969), p. 55. See also pp. 53, 129. The Puritans usually used the words emblem, type, sign, or similitude to refer to what most modern literary critics have defined as symbol. Dickran and Ann Tashjian have noted that the

In 1674 Joshua Moody, assistant pastor at the First Church, preached the election sermon in Boston, using the common figure of human existence as a war and finding in the technical commands of the parade ground and in the movements and accoutrements of battle a wealth of spiritual significance put there by God. He explained the figurative method as the best way to speak of God in the language of men, as indeed the way that God Himself chooses: "As for my manner of speaking in the using of many Metaphorical Expressions, and Allusions unto the Calling, Postures, and motions of Soldiers...I conceive a man should take Measure of his theme to cut out his Language by, and make it up something according to the mode of his Auditory." Since his theme was the spiritual significance of secular callings, Moody was careful to point out that God was constantly "spiritualizing all our Employments" and that his own use of figures was not presumptuous creation, but merely an explication of God's method. "From the King upon the Throne to the Hewer of wood and drawer of water, the Lord is in his Word teaching us by such familiar and known *Metaphors* taken from those Callings that we are versed in."[3] For Moody as for the others, the transcendent God had condescended to treat on man's level, had chosen to be

interplay "between allegory and emblem was often so fluid as to render hard distinctions arbitrary," *Memorials for Children of Change: The Art of Early New England Stonecarving* (Middletown, Conn., 1974), p. 168. In *The Puritan Origins of the American Self* (New Haven, Conn., 1975), Sacvan Bercovitch has clearly detailed the changing nature of these distinctions in tracing the development of Puritan typology from an orthodox "hermeneutical mode connecting the Old Testament to the New," p. 35, to a more widely applied "typology of current affairs" that "we would now call symbolic interpretation," p. 113. The word "symbol" in our modern sense was first used by Spenser and appeared quite rarely in seventeenth-century writings; its meaning was usually approximated by one of the words listed above, all of which appeared far more often (*OED*).

[2]See Perry Miller's statement of the originality of Jonathan Edwards' worldview in the introduction to his edition of Edwards' *Images or Shadows of Divine Things* (New Haven, Conn., 1948), p. 7, and Ursula Brumm, *American Thought and Religious Typology*, trans. John Hoaglund (New Brunswick, N.J., 1970), p. 98. Edwards is quoted from *Images or Shadows of Divine Things*, p. 44. Taylor's Meditation I, Second Series, is quoted from *The Poems of Edward Taylor*, ed. Donald E. Stanford (New Haven, Conn., 1960), p. 83.

[3]Joshua Moody, *Souldiery Spiritualized* (Cambridge, Mass., 1674), in Perry Miller and Thomas H. Johnson, eds., *The Puritans* (1938; rev. ed., New York, 1963), I, 367-68.

immanent in the world in forms that man could understand. Though they steered a middle course between complete anthropomorphism and complete unintelligibility, the Puritans steered rather closer to the former than has been commonly believed. The world they inhabited, no less than the Bible from which they tried to draw the pattern for the perfect church and society, was a communication from God, to be studied closely and explicated accurately. Though its abuse could lead them from Him, its proper religious use was a "plain man's pathway to heaven." It offered the poet a world rich in intrinsic symbols, correspondences, and significances that were not decorations but necessary parts of the truth he attempted to tell.

One way in which the Puritan used the world in his quest for heaven was in religious meditation. Norman Grabo has recognized that "the art of Puritan devotion was basically a method for channeling emotion into verbal structures—a poetic method."[4] Meditation was a central concern for English and American Puritans throughout the seventeenth century, and the meditational handbooks used by the Puritans dealt with the essentially literary problem of using verbal methods to arouse and express emotion. So close were meditation and poetry in Puritan thinking that Anne Bradstreet entitled one of her best long poems "Contemplations," Philip Pain entitled his only extant poems *Daily Meditations,* and Edward Taylor referred to the poems written at monthly intervals for over forty-four years as "Preparatory Meditations." To understand Puritan poetry, and the attitudes toward the world, imagery, and language that inform it, we must examine this system of ideas and attitudes that stood so closely and clearly behind it.

Histories of Catholic meditational practices and of Puritan meditation after Baxter have been well told and require no detailed repetition here. Until the beginning of the seventeenth

---

[4]See Norman S. Grabo, "The Veiled Vision: The Role of Aesthetics in Early American Intellectual History," *William and Mary Quarterly,* 3rd Ser., 19 (1962), 493-510; "The Art of Puritan Devotion," *Seventeenth-Century News,* 26 (1968), 7-9; "John Cotton's Aesthetics: A Sketch," *Early American Literature,* 3 (1968), 4-10; and "Puritan Devotion and American Literary History," in *Themes and Directions in American Literature: Essays in Honor of Leon Howard,* ed. Ray B. Browne and Donald Pizer (Lafayette, Ind., 1969), pp. 6-23. Grabo is quoted from "The Art of Puritan Devotion," p. 9.

century, most works on meditation were written by Catholics and brought into England by the Jesuits. From these early writings on, the function of meditation was to arouse the affections and to bring the Christian into more intimate emotional relation with his God. In his *Introduction to the Devout Life,* St. Francis de Sales defined meditation: "When we think of heavenly things, not to learn but to love them, that is called to meditate: and the exercise thereof, Meditation."[5] St. Ignatius Loyola provided a relentlessly structured method for the arousal of his love in his *Spiritual Exercises.* The "Exercitant," as Loyola called the person meditating, was to exercise in sequence three faculties of his soul — memory, understanding, and will. Subject matter for the meditation, *e.g.,* doctrine, Scriptural incident, or some object with spiritual significance, was called up by memory, and one first attempted to get as detailed and vivid an apprehension of it as he could using only his memory and imagination. Then one exercised one's understanding, or reason, upon the image or proposition supplied by memory until, after thorough intellectual examination, the work of understanding was complete. Only then did the exercitant judge the subject and submit it to his will and affections, which were moved to great joy or sorrow. Meditation drove dogma into imagination, enlivened doctrine into thoroughly apprehended truth.

Among Puritans this formerly Catholic method of spiritual exercise received quick and wide acceptance. Answering in 1589 the charge (made by the Jesuit Robert Persons) that the English had no devotional writers, Edmund Bunny contended that the Reformers were reading handbooks of meditation. By 1628 they

[5]For a discussion of the meditative tradition and its influence on English poetry, see Louis L. Martz, *The Poetry of Meditation,* rev. ed. (1954; New Haven, Conn., 1962). Martz asserted that structured meditation became a concern of the Puritans only after 1650, after Baxter had made palatable to them methods of meditation that were essentially Catholic. That Baxter was not nearly so original as he claimed to be has been demonstrated by Norman Grabo in "Puritan Devotion and American Literary History," p. 12. Grabo discussed the importation into England of Catholic handbooks on meditation in *Edward Taylor* (New Haven, Conn., 1961), p. 60. For a discussion of Puritan meditation after Baxter, see U. Milo Kaufmann, *The Pilgrim's Progress and Traditions in Puritan Meditation* (New Haven, Conn., 1966). St. Francis de Sales is quoted in Louis L. Martz, *The Poetry of Meditation,* p. 15.

were writing them. In that year, the English Puritan minister Thomas Taylor published his *Meditations from the Creatures,* "as it was preached in Aldermanbury." "I thought fit to afford a little help, to lead up careful Christians into this mount of Meditation: in which mount God will be seen." Though "the Lord himself, his Word and Decrees, are the principal object of ordinary Meditation," Taylor wished to extend traditional meditation to include among its objects images drawn from the sensible world. He suggests that "so are his works and execution of his decrees a fit object" and cites the example of David, who "acknowledgeth himself occupied in contemplation of the heavens and stars...that he is led to God by them." The relationship between God and the world, then, is not dualistic but hierarchical. God is an author, and the world is His book, to be read by man and not despised, mistrusted, or ignored: "The world is his book; so many pages, as so many several creatures; no page is empty, but full of lines; every quality of the creature, is a several letter of this book, and no letter without a part of God's wisdom in it."

If the world itself is metaphorical, then "the voice of the Creatures is not be banished out of the church," and ministers must be metaphorical in their conceivings and their preachings: "If all Scriptures be profitable to teach and improve, then those that teach divine things from natural." This metaphorical method had Biblical sanction, since "the Prophets and Apostles, and Christ himself were most in this kind of instruction, by Parables and Similitudes: therefore Ministers and Pastors may do the like."

In focusing on the metaphorical nature of the physical world and the metaphorical language of the Bible, Taylor was moving toward an understanding of meditation as a literary, as well as a religious, exercise, and he knew it. Discussing metaphorical predications about the nature of God, he clearly moves into the realm of literary criticism: "Hands and fingers are ascribed to God metaphorically. And here the heavens are called not the works of his hands, but his fingers: to note his singular industry, his exquisite workmanship and art, and also special love and care." For Thomas Taylor, then, meditation from the creatures lifted one's thoughts and affections to God, not by denying the physical world, but by reflecting on it in words, by translating God's physical metaphors into verbal metaphors. The world was a text, a system of metaphors, a language, a voice, and Taylor concluded his treatise with an appropriate Latin tag: *"Vox Dei est in omnibus, per omnia, de omnibus et ad omnia, loquens nobiscum semper et ubique."* In the third edition (London, 1632) of this popular book, he provided his own translation: "The voice of Goᴅ in all the creatures and by them all speaketh unto us always and everywhere." The sensible world was part of the word—a voice to be heeded, a book to be read—and meditation was a verbal, a literary method of practicing one's religion.[6]

For the Puritans who later came to America, as for Thomas Taylor, meditation was a verbal method of taking a truth from the physical world or of giving life to a truth already understood intellectually by driving it home to the affections, to the nerve ends. In *The Soules Preparation for Christ* (London, 1632), Thomas Hooker defined meditation: "It is a settled exercise for two ends: first to make a further inquiry of the truth: and secondly, to make the heart affected therewith." That Hooker's meditative technique was metaphorical is clear from his examples: "It is with meditation as it is with usurers that will grate upon men, and grind the faces of the poor, and suck the blood of the needy, they will exact upon men. ...So doth meditation, it exacts and slayeth the soul of a poor sinner, you have committed adultery in a corner but you shall not carry it away."[7] For Hooker, the language appropriate to meditation was concrete, imagistic, and metaphoric because this kind of charged language would affect the heart. It was not only possible for meditation to use such language, linking the invisible things of God with the visible things of this world—the holy practice of meditation with the cruelty of usurers—it was necessary; it was commanded.[8]

---

[6]Thomas Taylor, *A Man in Christ, or: A new CREATURE. To which is added a Treatise, containing Meditations from the CREATURES* (London, 1628), pp. 2, 5-8, 23, 104.

[7]Thomas Hooker, *The Soules Preparation for Christ, or A Treatise of Contrition* (London, 1632), pp. 84-86.

[8]Indeed, the Puritan dependence upon language and upon literary metaphors *(e.g.* the creatures are letters in a book written by God) was so great that they could not comprehend a religion based upon "visions and magic" rather than upon words. See Frank Shuffelton, "Indian Devils and Pilgrim Fathers: Squanto, Hobomok, and the English Conception of Indian Religion," *New England Quarterly,* 49 (March 1976), 109-116.

Early in his career, for example, young John Cotton wrote that "a man that is enlightened with the knowledge of God's will, and the mystery of Salvation; may lawfully in his meditations make use of diverse Creatures or Things, that are apt and fit to represent Spiritual things unto him."[9] In 1648 the *Shorter Catechism* of the Westminster Assembly, a work which exerted a pervasive influence among Puritans, made the practice of meditation a duty, a necessary part of preparing oneself for the Lord's Supper. However, the most pervasive influence on Puritan meditational practices and the poetry they informed was a book published in England in January 1649/50, Richard Baxter's *The Saints' Everlasting Rest,* a work so influential among Puritans that until recently scholars assumed that it was the first Puritan treatise on meditation and ignored its predecessors.

Well qualified to succeed in making acceptable to his fellow Protestants Catholic methods of devotion, Baxter had sided early with the Puritan cause and had served as a military chaplain in the Parliamentary armies during the Civil War. Though he contributed to the Restoration, he turned down the bishopric that would have been his reward and suffered sufficiently under Charles II and James II to qualify for popular investiture as living Protestant martyr. In 1659 he was to publish *A Key for Catholicks, to open the jugling of the Jesuits,* a work which would have cleared him of the charge of being soft on Catholics, had anyone thought to make it. His *Saints' Everlasting Rest* appeared almost exactly one year after the execution of Charles I. Nine editions in twelve years bespeak a ready audience. Called by one scholar "one of the most popular Puritan books of the entire seventeenth century" and the major book of a man whose "various works were common to the libraries of both New England and the southern

---

[9]Drawing the customary distinction between the legitimate act of *seeing* the symbols that God had put in one's way and the idolatrous act of *making* them, Cotton continued: "but he must not take upon him to determine them to be used as signs for such an end and purpose." Written early in his career, these statements were later published as *Some Treasure Fetched out of Rubbish* (London, 1660), p. 29 and are quoted by Grabo, "Puritan Devotion," pp. 19-20. Cotton more than Hooker feared the possibility of idolatry lurking in the religious use of images, but even he acknowledged the value of meditation on the creatures and believed that if one kept clear the distinction between seeing signs and making them, one would be safe.

colonies,"[10] Baxter's enormous tome was intended as a guidebook for the Puritan's journey to heaven. The most important part of that journey was meditation; hence the most important part of Baxter's book was "The Fourth Part. Containing a Directory for the getting and keeping of the Heart in Heaven: By the diligent practice of that Excellent unknown Deity of *Heavenly Meditation*. Being the main thing intended by the Author, in the writing of this Book; and to which all the rest is but subservient." In this section of one of the most popular and influential of Puritan books, Baxter repeated several themes in Thomas Taylor's *Meditations from the Creatures* and brought together most of the attitudes that made Puritan poetry possible: the positive approach to the sensible world, the recognition that though the senses were potentially dangerous they had their part in worship, the rationale for the use of sensuous imagery drawn from the creatures to describe the invisible things of God, and a complex but consistent statement of the uses and limits of language in meditation.

Baxter began by insisting on the centrality of meditation to the holy life: "All that I have said is but for the preparation to this: The Doctrinal part is but to instruct you to this: the rest of the uses are but introductions to this." Primary among "Some Advantages and Helps for raising and Affecting the Soul by this Meditation" were the senses and their objects. Baxter's detailed discussion of them made explicit many of the complex but consistent attitudes implicit in Puritan poetry.

> Why sure it will be a point of our Spiritual Prudence, and a singular help to the furthering of the work of Faith to call in our sense to our assistance: if we can make friends of these usual enemies, and make them instruments of raising us to God, which are the usual means of drawing us from God, I think we shall perform a very excellent work. Surely it is both possible and lawful, yea, and necessary too, to do something in this kind: for God would not have given us either our Senses themselves, or their usual objects, if they might not have been serviceable to his own Praise, and helps to raise us to the apprehension of higher things.

Though they recognized the potential dangers of the senses, Puritans could use them in religious meditation and therefore

---

[10]Martz, *The Poetry of Meditation*, p. 154, and Louis B. Wright, *The Cultural Life of the American Colonies 1607-1763* (New York, 1957), p. 140.

in the literature that recorded that meditation. Like all things worldly, the senses trapped men who thought that there was nothing beyond them, but they, again like all things worldly, had a proper use. Indeed, even God used them when revealing himself to man through Scripture.

> And it is very considerable how the holy Ghost doth condescend in the phrase of Scripture, in bringing things down to the reach of sense; how he sets forth the excellencies of Spiritual things in words that are borrowed from the objects of sense; how he describeth the glory of the New *Jerusalem,* in expressions that might take even with flesh itself: As that the Streets and Buildings are pure Gold, that the gates are Pearl...That we shall eat and drink with Christ at his Table in his Kingdom: that he will drink with us the fruit of the Vine new; that we shall shine as the Sun in the Firmament of our Father: These with most other descriptions of our Glory are expressed, as if it were to the very flesh and Sense; which though they are all improper and figurative, yet doubtless if such expressions had not been best, and to us necessary, the Holy Ghost would not have so frequently used them.

Baxter's tone here was insistent; he realized that he had to make his case, to assure his readers that he was not urging them to become merely men of sense. But, he did make the case, as the many examples of sensuous expression of spiritual truths testify.

For Baxter, who wrote poetry, as for the American Willard, God had condescended to treat on man's level in His use of figurative language, and that condescension compelled an appropriate response from man. "He that will speak to man's understanding must speak in man's language, and speak that which he is capable to conceive. And doubtless as the Spirit doth speak, so we must hear; and if our necessity cause him to condescend in his expressions, it must needs cause us to be low in our conceivings." Indeed the central and defining event in Christianity, the Incarnation of the invisible God in visible man was, like creation and all other metaphor, God's act of making part of Himself available to the understanding of man. "It is one reason of Christ's assuming and continuing our nature with the Godhead, that we might know him the better, when he is so much nearer to us: and we might have more positive conceivings of him, and so our minds might have familiarity with him, who before was quite beyond their reach." Baxter was, of course, aware of the dangers of idolatry (into which he asserted the Catholics had fallen) and of the limits of language. He realized that an anthropomorphic view of God and heaven was a psychic necessity, not a metaphysical fact:

> But what is my scope in all this? is it that we might think Heaven to be made of Gold and Pearl? or that we should picture Christ, as the Papists do, in such a shape? or that we should think Saints and Angels do indeed eat and drink? No, not that we should take the Spirit's figurative expressions to be meant according to strict propriety: or have fleshy conceivings of spiritual things, so as to believe them to be such indeed: But this; to think that to conceive or speak of them in strict propriety, is utterly beyond our reach and capacity: and therefore we must conceive of them as we are able; and that the Spirit would not have represented them in these notions to us, but that we have no better notions to apprehend them by; and therefore that we can make use of these phrases of the Spirit to quicken our apprehensions and affections.

Correspondences between the invisible things of God and the visible things of earth exist by fiat of God and can be expressed only through some form of figuration. Though these figures do not express God and heaven as such are known by God Himself and by those saints who are with Him in heaven, they do express as much of the beatific vision as man on earth can and needs to know. Limited and potentially dangerous, they are hardly to be scorned by mortal man.

In Baxter's prose, then, we find the theological rationale for the figures that constitute so much of Puritan religious poetry. We find here the explicit statement of the attitude that enabled Puritan poets to delight in the sensible world, to state its vanities only in comparison with the joys of God and heaven, and to use the former to figure the latter. Even God had taken upon Himself the attributes of man, and though to afford a direct picture of Him would certainly have been idolatrous, as both Baxter and Willard had warned, nevertheless, man could understand and speak of and love God as anthropomorphically as God had "accommodated" His revelations to the temporary, earthly understandings of His creatures. Having justified the uses of figuration to describe things spiritual, Baxter concluded: "The like may be said of those expressions of God in Scripture, wherein he represents himself in the imperfections of creatures, as anger, repenting, willing what shall not come to pass, etc." They are "improper, drawn from the manner of man," but "we can see no better yet."[11]

Baxter made explicit the Puritan attitudes toward the sensible world, the religious use of images drawn from it, and the limits and necessity of figurative language based on that imagery. These attitudes were far more pervasive and uniform than a doctrinaire pluralist would expect. Though the Puritans neither wrote an explicit *ars poetica* nor, like Blake and Yeats, constructed their world-view in order to provide symbols for poetry, their world-view was positive, symbolic, and therefore far more conducive to the production of poetry than the world-view hitherto imputed to them. The poetics implicit in their prose writings avoided the worship, not the making, of images. Based on the belief that the world was the gift of a loving God, it comprised many paeans to the beauty and abundance of the natural world, a world perceived both as an *a fortiori* argument for the beauty and goodness of God and as a God-wrought system of symbols intended to lead man to heaven. Puritans believed that meaning resided in the symbolic world itself, and their poetics has far more in common with the Latin concept of the poet as *vates* ("seer"), one who sees and says the truth, than with the Greek concept of the poet as *poeta* ("maker"), one who creates verbal artifacts. We may use the critical tools provided by the New Critical view of the poem as verbal artifact in our reading of Puritan poetry, but it is clear that the making of such artifacts was not their intention when they wrote it: their avowed task was simply to say, to utter, the truth they saw.

The sensible world, the senses, the words used to arouse and describe the meanings and affections appropriate to them, all were limited but necessary; all had their parts to play in salvation. Though not the ultimate object of man's love, they were

[11]Richard Baxter, *The Saints' Everlasting Rest,* 9th ed. (London, pp. 694, 749-51. Where before he had recognized the dangers of idolatry, Baxter now noted the dangers of dealing only in religious abstractions: "Go to then; When thou settest thyself to meditate on the Joys above, think on them boldly as Scripture hath expressed them; Bring down thy conceivings to the reach of sense. ...Both Love, and Joy are promoted by familiar acquaintance: When we go to think of God and Glory in proper conceivings without these spectacles, we are lost and have nothing to fix our thoughts upon" (p. 751).

created by God out of His love for man in order to give man a suitable object for his earthly love. Puritan poets, like all Puritans, knew that if they were to pass to the next world they must turn their attention from the unmixed love of this one. Ultimately less real than God and heaven, this world had, nonetheless, both its delights and its uses.[12]

[12]Nowhere is this love clearer, and nowhere is the distance between the Puritan and the Gnostic or Manichaean or Catharist dualist greater than in their attitudes toward the death of the body. The Catharists, for example, believed that the proper life of man on earth consisted of the *endura,* ritual suicide by starvation. But the Puritans did not despise the body, nor were they half in love with easeful death. Though neoplatonic in some respects, the Puritans saw the body as something more than the prison from which the soul should happily escape at its first opportunity. Samuel Willard wrote of death: "It makes a separation between the soul and body. This is the very nature of it, and is in itself a misery; and for that reason the Godly themselves have a natural reluctancy against it; they would not pass through it if they could go to heaven without it." Samuel Willard, *A Compleat Body of Divinity in Two Hundred and Fifty Expository Lectures on the Assembly's Shorter Catechism* (Boston, 1726), p. 233. David E. Stannard has presented considerable evidence "that the Puritans were gripped individually and collectively by an intense and unremitting fear of death." See "Death and Dying in Puritan New England," *American Historical Review,* 78 (1973), 1315.

Israel in Babylon:
The Archetype of the Captivity Narratives

by Richard Slotkin

Almost from the moment of its literary genesis, the New England Indian captivity narrative functioned as a myth, reducing the Puritan state of mind and world view, along with the events of colonization and settlement, into archetypal drama. In it a single individual, usually a woman, stands passively under the strokes of evil, awaiting rescue by the grace of God. The sufferer represents the whole, chastened body of Puritan society; and the temporary bondage of the captive to the Indian is dual paradigm—of the bondage of the soul to the flesh and to the temptations arising from original sin, and of the self-exile of the English Israel from England. In the Indian's devilish clutches, the captive had to meet and reject the temptation of Indian marriage and/or the Indian's "cannibal" Eucharist. To partake of the Indian's love or of his equivalent of bread and wine was to debase, to un-English the very soul. The captive's ultimate redemption by the grace of Christ and the efforts of the Puritan magistrates is likened to the regeneration of the soul in conversion. The ordeal is at once threatful of pain and evil and promising of ultimate salvation. Through the captive's proxy, the promise of a similar salvation could be offered to the faithful among the reading public, while the captive's torments remained to harrow the hearts of those not yet awakened to their fallen nature. This is the pattern suggested by Underhill in his account of the captive maids, whose condition he likens to that of "captive Israel" and whose adventure is presented as a parable of the colonists' collective salvation-through-affliction.[1]

The first captivity narratives were genuine, first-person accounts of actual ordeals, and for that reason it is possible to view the genre as a natural, spontaneous product of the New World experience. However, Puritan ministers and men of letters were quick to realize the polemical and theological potential in the tales and began to exercise direct control over the composition of the narratives, shaping them for their own ends. Under their hands, the genre became very flexible, serving (often simultaneously) as literary entertainment, material for revival sermons, vehicle for political diatribes, and "experimental" evidence in philosophical and theological works. The great and continuing popularity of these narratives, the uses to which they were put, and the nature of the symbolism employed in them are evidence that the captivity narratives constitute the first coherent myth-literature developed in America for American audiences. The nature and extent of the captivity narratives' popularity is attested by the fact that they completely dominate the list of frontier narratives published in America between 1680 and 1716,* replacing narratives of soldierly exploits in the sermon-narrative literature.[2] It almost seems as if the only experience of intimacy with the Indians that New England readers would accept was the experience of the captive (and possibly that of the missionary). Even after 1720 the tales of captivity continued to be popular, although they shared the market with other types of narrative; and the first tentative American efforts at short fiction and the "first American novel" (Brown's *Edgar Huntly*) were very much in the vein of the captivity narratives.

*Land-promotion brochures and legal documents also appeared in profusion throughout the period but did not have the imaginative charge of the narrative literature.

[1]John Underhill, *Newes from America* (London, 1638), in *Collections of the Massachusetts Historical Society,* 3d ser. 6 (1837), pp. 19, 18.

[2]See Roy Harvey Pearce, "The Significances of the Captivity Narrative," *American Literature,* 19 (March 1949), 1-20. See also Robert William Glenroie Vail, *The Voice of the Old Frontier* (Philadelphia: Univ. of Pennsylvania Press, 1949), pp. 167-218, and Frank Luther Mott, *Golden Multitudes* (New York: Macmillan, 1947), pp. 303-5.

The first and perhaps the best of the captivity narratives was Mary Rowlandson's *The Soveraignty and Goodness of God, Together with the Faithfulness of His Promises Displayed: Being a Narrative of the Captivity and Restauration of Mrs. Mary Rowlandson,* first published in 1682. Mrs. Rowlandson's narrative is, in the sense in which I have defined the term, an archetype—that is, the initiator of a genre of narrative within American culture, the primary model of which all subsequent captivities are diminished copies, or types. This is not the same as the Jungian definition of an archetype as a narrative which is at once a cultural phenomenon and an organic component of the individual mind; nor is it the pancultural ur-narrative, or monomyth, described by Campbell in *Hero with a Thousand Faces* and by Frazer in his discussion of the primitive myths of the divine king. If Jung is right, her narrative is reducible to the common terms of a universally internalized mythology. Certainly the terms of her narrative, its structure and its symbolism, are derived from older European mythologies, which in turn derive from still more primitive Biblical and Indo-European myths. She frequently acknowledges her debt by using Biblical stories as archetypes and precedents for her own situation. However, it is the purpose of this study, not to trace these myths to some primeval source, whether in a collective unconscious or a primitive Indo-European root-culture, but rather to trace the evolution of particularized myths as they function within the history of a single culture. In this limited context, Mrs. Rowlandson's narrative functions as an archetype, creating a paradigm of personal and collective history that can be discerned as an informing structure throughout Puritan and (with modifications) in later American narrative literature. It was the captivity narrative that provided the effective means of assimilating the colonial inheritance of primitive and European-Christian mythology to the circumstances of American life, of making the universal mythology applicable to a special cultural situation.

The internal coherence of the captivity-based mythology as a representation of personal and collective history, its breadth and depth of influence in New England thought and literature, and its long-term maintenance of its evocative power can be suggested by comparing Mrs. Rowlandson's narrative with other key documents of the Puritan canon. Bunyan's allegory of the soul's quest and pilgrimage in *Pilgrim's Progress* and the emigration tracts of Bradford and John White are useful for suggesting the relevance of the captivity of the Puritans' vision of their life pattern, their quest, and their historical emigration from England. Michael Wigglesworth's *Day of Doom* (1662), the classic Puritan vision of the apocalypse and judgment, also offers suggestive parallels with the captivity myth. And Jonathan Edwards's "Sinners in the Hands of an Angry God" (1749)—the archetypal revival sermon by the most subtle student of the psychology of personal conversion—suggests the relevance of the captivity to the psychology of conversion. Analogies between the captivity and Edwards's sermon are especially interesting because of his "sensationalist" rhetoric: the sermon is designed to impose a series of sense perceptions on the hearer, which will bypass or overwhelm the defenses of his corrupted reason and operate directly on his "affections," thus carrying him into the emotional crisis of religious conversion. This is precisely the way in which myth-tales (such as Mrs. Rowlandson's) operate on their audiences; and the success of Edwards's sermons is testimony to the evocative power of the captivity-myth imagery.

Mrs. Rowlandson's captivity begins typically, with the heroine-victim in a state of relatively complacent ease. She is only vaguely troubled by her easy situation, vaguely wondering why God does not "try" her in some way. Others of her acquaintance have been so tried, and some have fallen; the Bible promises that all will be tried and should be prepared. Presumably her minister-husband reminds his wife and the community of this each Sunday. But there is only the vaguest suspense or anticipation of threatening evil in the community or in Mrs. Rowlandson's heart. Somehow the victim has forgotten the true meaning of these warnings and portents, believing that the sword will always be kept from the family. She takes peace for granted, but as a good Puritan she longs for some "affliction" of God to be visited upon her, in order that her sinful will might be overborne by a stronger and purer force of holiness than her own. Like Underhill's prospective emigrants, she views the holy afflictions of her fellow Saints in the wilderness and in her complacency thinks (in Underhill's words), "Would I had some of those." In so doing she tempts God, committing the sin of pride, failing to realize what the experience of God's wrath might be, and believing herself capable of sustaining it:

> Before I knew what affliction meant, I was ready sometimes to wish for it. When I lived in prosperity, having the comforts of the world about me,...and yet seeing many (whom I preferred before myself) under many trials and afflictions, in sickness, weakness, poverty, losses, crosses, and cares of the world, I should be sometimes jealous lest I should have my portion in this life.... Hebrews xii. 6, *For Whom the Lord loveth he chastiseth, and scourgeth every son whom he receiveth.*[3]

Implicit in this point of view is the fear of the double-edged promise of the New World: the opulent rewards, which might make the spirit too secure and unready for the test, and the freedom from artificial restraints, which placed the whole weight of responsibility for the maintenance of virtue in thought and action on the lonely individual. Yet it was for this very reason that the Puritan emigrants had come to America, seeking a hard way to do the Lord's work, not (as their critics charged) fleeing the holy war to live in greater ease. Thomas Shepard, John White, William Bradford, and all the other Puritan emigration tractarians emphasized the arduousness of the task, the ascetic and self-mortifying spirit of the emigrants. Not the "pleasure, profits and honors of the world," but the trials and pains of a land ruled by "death, the king of terror," is their dwelling-place.[4] Like Bunyan's Christian, they must take unto themselves a painful "cross" and love it more than "the treasures of Egypt."[5] Similarly the captivity experience, with its pains and trials, brings a forced end to comforts and pleasures. The cross is thrust upon the Chris-

[3] Mary Rowlandson, *The Soveraignty and Goodness of God, Together with the Faithfulness of His Promises Displayed: Being a Narrative of the Captivity and Restauration of Mrs. Mary Rowlandson,* in *Narratives of the Indian Wars: 1675-1699,* ed. Charles Henry Lincoln (New York: Barnes and Noble, 1966), pp. 166-67.

[4] William Bradford, *Of Plymouth Plantation,* ed. Samuel Eliot Morison (New York: Modern Library, 1967), pp. 23-27; Thomas Shepard, "Defense of the Answer," in *The Puritans,* ed. Perry Miller and Thomas H. Johnson, 2 vols., rev. ed. (New York: Harper and Row, Harper Torchbooks, 1963), 1:120-21.

[5] John Bunyan, *Pilgrim's Progress,* ed. Louis Martz (New York: Holt, Rinehart, and Winston, Rinehart Editions, 1965), p. 23.

tian—to love it, accept it, and be saved; or to rail against it and perish.

The situation of the Puritan soul, for all its outward security, is thus extremely precarious. His farm is rich, and the landscape is bright and open, but it sits on the brink of the abysmal woods, within whose shadows devilish Indians move. Surrounded by his fellows, he knows that at the ultimate judgment he must stand alone—that even now, when he faces God within his conscience, he is solitary. The world seems secure, but apocalypse lies just below the surface of the mind, of the world. When the moment of judgment or conversion or massacre comes, this latent truth becomes manifest. The sinner beholds his sinfulness; the already damned, the fact of damnation; the backslidden frontiersman, the physical form of his degeneration. Thus Edwards takes as his text the line "Their foot shall slide in due time" and reads it as a prophecy:

> [The wicked] ...were always exposed to *destruction;* As one who walks in slippery places is every moment liable to fall. ...That the reason why they are not fallen already, and do not fall now, is only that God's appointed time is not come. For it is said, that when that due time...comes, *their foot shall slide.* Then they shall be left to fall, as they are inclined by their own weight...as he that stands on such slippery declining ground, on the edge of a pit, he cannot stand alone, when he is let go he immediately falls and is lost.[6]

The good, beloved land on which they walk and the very air they breathe are seen as perilous, embodying an implacable hostility toward themselves. The land and creatures they believed they had conquered and tamed are still in the hands of God, ready to turn and visit his judgment upon them:

> Were it not for the sovereign pleasure of God, the earth would not bear you for one moment; for you are a burden to it; the creation groans with you; the creature is made subject to the bondage of your corruption, not willingly; the sun does not willingly shine upon you to give you light to serve sin and Satan; the earth does not willingly yield her increase to satsify your lusts. ...And the

[6]Jonathan Edwards, "Sinners in the Hands of an Angry God," in *Representative Selections,* ed. Charles Faust and Thomas H. Johnson (New York: Hill and Wang, 1962), pp. 155-56.

world would spew you out, were it not for the sovereign hand of
him who hath subjected it in hope.[7]

The advent of judgment, of conversion, or of captivity breaks
into the troubled complacency of the consciousness with sudden
violence, catching the soul unprepared. Wigglesworth's poetic
vision of the "Day of Doom" employs the same imagery and pattern of events as Mrs. Rowlandson:

> Still was the Night, Serene and Bright, when all Men sleeping lay;
> Calm was the season, and carnal reason thought so twould last for ay.
> Soul, take thine ease, let sorrow cease, much good thou hast in store;
> This was their Song, their Cups among, the Evening before.

Edwards's exemplary "natural man" sings the same song, depending "upon himself for his own security," in his stored-up
good works, instead of forgetting himself and depending upon
the person of Christ. As Wigglesworth shows, such egocentric
dreams are disrupted suddenly, without warning, violently:

> For at midnight brake forth a Light, which turned the night to day,
> And speedily an hideous cry did all the world dismay.
> Sinners awake, their hearts do ake, trembling their loynes surprizeth;
> Amaz'd with fear, by what they hear, each one of them ariseth.
>
> Straightway appears (they see't with tears) the Son of God most dread;
> Who with his Train comes on amain to Judge both Quick and Dead.[8]

Mrs. Rowlandson likewise is caught all unprepared, roused from
her bed by the advent of a judgment. The hideous cries of the
savages, the sounds of battle, and the sight of several houses burning amaze her with fear: "When we are in prosperity, Oh, the
little that we think of such dreadfull sights, and to see our dear
Friends, and Relations bleeding out their heart blood upon the
ground." Yet these sights are but the outward manifestations of
a divine judgment; behind the faces of King Philip and his horde
of savages, she discerns "the Son of God most dread": "Oh the
dolefull sight that now was to behold at this House! *Come behold
the works of the Lord, what dissolations he has made in the Earth*

---

[7] Ibid., pp. 162-63.

[8] Michael Wigglesworth, "The Day of Doom," in *Colonial American Writing,* ed. Roy Harvey Pearce (New York: Holt, Rinehart, and Winston; Rinehart
Editions, 1964), pp. 233-34.

[Psalm 46:8] ."[9] Like the sinners in Wigglesworth's poem, she is unready for her ordeal:

> I had often before this said, that if the Indians should come, I should chuse rather to be killed by them then taken alive, but when it came to the tryal my mind changed; their glittering weapons so daunted my spirit, that I chose to go along with those (as I may say) ravenous Beasts, then that moment to end my dayes.[10]

The larger patterns of the apocalypse and captivity are also present in the Puritan conception of the individual conversion experience as detailed by Edwards. Judgment for salvation or damnation comes without warning, catching will and consciousness asleep. If we could speak with the damned who have experienced judgment, says Edwards, they would give the following account (which repeats, in its essentials, the pattern of the captivity):

> No, I never intended to come here [to hell] : I had laid out matters otherwise in my mind; I thought I should contrive well for myself: ... I intended to take effectual care; but it came upon me unexpected; I did not look for it at that time, and in that manner; it came as a thief: Death outwitted me: God's wrath was too quick for me. Oh, my cursed foolishness! I was flattering myself and pleasing myself with vain dreams of what I would do hereafter; and when I was saying, Peace and safety, then suddenly destruction came upon me.[11]

Edwards saw the use or application of his sermon as the "awakening" of "unconverted persons in this congregation" to their actual condition, their real solitude and helpless nakedness in the cold eye of God. This same awakening is achieved for Mary Rowlandson at the advent of the Indians, as it is for Wigglesworth's sinners at the advent of Christ. They are immediately plunged into isolation. Family ties, above all, are violently disrupted; and the essence of their trial is whether they can accept this judgmental disruption as the work of God's grace. Mrs. Rowlandson's elder sister cannot: "Seeing those wofull sights, the Infidels haling Mothers one way, and Children another, and

---

[9] *Soveraignty and Goodness of God,* p. 120.
[10] Ibid., p. 121.
[11] "Sinners in the Hands of an Angry God," pp. 160-61.

some wallowing in their blood: and her elder Son telling her that her Son William was dead, and my self wounded, she said, And, Lord, let me dy with them; which was no sooner said, but she was struck with a Bullet, and fell down dead over the threshold."[12]

The breaking of family ties continues and is progressively intensified throughout the narrative, leaving Mrs. Rowlandson increasingly isolated. Her wounded baby dies after some days of torment, her son is separated from her, and she herself is carried further into the wilderness. The Indians assure her that they will waylay and kill her husband, who had been in Boston during the attack on Lancaster, if he comes to seek her. She stands alone in her trial, and the first test imposed on her is that she accept her isolation and her family's destruction as God's will.

The trial is identical with that imposed on Bunyan's pilgrim, Christian, who must desert his wife and children to be tried by his God, obeying the biblical injunction: "If any man come to me, and hate not his father, and mother, and wife, and children, and brethren, and sisters, yea, and his own life also, he cannot be my disciple."[13] Thomas Shepard, justifying the Puritan emigration to hostile stay-at-homes, presents the New England adventure in terms of the same injunction:

> When wee looke back and consider what a strange poise of spirit the Lord hath laid upon many of our hearts, wee cannot but wonder at ourselves, that so many, and some so weak and tender, with such cheerfulnesse and constant resolutions against so many perswasions of friends, discouragements from the ill report of this Countrey... yet should leave our accomodations and comforts, should foresake our dearest relations, Parents, brethren, Sisters, Christian friends ...and all this to go to a wildernesse.[14]

Mrs. Rowlandson, echoing the language of both passages, laments the destruction of her family but is able to reconcile it with her vision of God's justice and the ordained condition of man:

> We had Husband and Father, and Children, and Sisters, and Friends, and Relations, and House, and Home, and many comforts of this Life: but now we may say, as Job, *Naked came I out of my*

[12]*Soveraignty and Goodness of God*, p. 120.
[13]*Pilgrim's Progress*, p. 23.
[14]"Defense of the Answer," p. 121.

Mothers Womb, and naked I shall return: The Lord gave, and the Lord hath taken away, Blessed be the Name of the Lord.[15]

Mrs. Rowlandson's captivity narrative does more than echo the literature of Puritanism and emigration. By the nature of its theme, setting, and structure, it comments on the "come-outer" tracts of White, Bradford, Winthrop, and Shepard. She dramatizes and brings to the surface the ambivalent feelings of desire (for emigration) and guilt (for "deserting" England)—feelings that undergulf the earlier writings—by casting her emigration as an unwilling captivity to heathens and by conceiving it not as a crusader's quest but as a sinner's trial and judgment. This vision provides her with an ethical code to sustain her in her trials. The captivity is an act of divine providence akin to God's "calling forth" of Abraham, Bunyan's Christian, and Shepard's Puritans. To question or rail against the breaking of the family is therefore to question the judgment of Jehovah himself. Yet it is humanly impossible not to lament the separation, misery, suffering, and death of loved ones. Mrs. Rowlandson's problem is the same as that of the "saved" in "The Day of Doom." The souls of men are brought alone before Christ the Judge, and "their own Consciences/ More proof give in of each Man's sin than thousand Witnesses." The bonds of the family are dissolved: the saved are forbidden to pity the damned, for "such compassion is out of fashion."[16]

The tender Mother will own no other of all her numerous brood
But such as stand at Christ's right hand acquitted through his Blood.
The pious Father had now much rather his graceless Son should lie
In Hell with Devils, for all his evils burning eternally.[17]

Mrs. Rowlandson, unlike her sister, accepts the judgment and its consequences: *"my Grace is sufficient for thee."* When her baby dies, she does not rail; rather, she thanks God for enabling her to bear her loss with the spirit of Job and concludes: "There I left that Child in the Wilderness, and must commit it, and myself also in this Wilderness-condition, to him who is above all."[18]

[15]*Soveraignty and Goodness of God*, p. 133.
[16]"The Day of Doom," pp. 248, 289-90.
[17]Ibid., pp. 289-90.
[18]*Soveraignty and Goodness of God,* pp. 120, 126.

The fact that the breakup of families is at the center of the trial by captivity suggests something of the state of the Puritan mind during the period of captivity narratives. The trauma of emigration centered on the emotional consequences of their leaving the ancestral English home voluntarily, doing violence to the ties of blood, friendship, and custom. Apologists like Shepard, Bradford, Winthrop, and White all attempted elaborate justifications of the act, which serve to underline their justifiable anxieties. But the captivity narratives invoked the criticism leveled at the first Puritans as admonitions to the American generations, bidding them keep the old ways and stay behind the "hedge" of settlement. These narratives imply that unwilling captivity is the only acceptable excuse for going into the wilderness—that the Puritans themselves were "captives" of the prelates, forced by them to leave a happy English home for a howling wilderness. The departure of the emigrants and Mrs. Rowlandson's acceptance of the butchery of her family are the American equivalents of Bunyan's Christian's farewell to his family, his shutting out their cries to return by putting "his fingers in his ears."[19] The crucial difference between Wigglesworth's division of the family into saved and damned and Mrs. Rowlandson's image of the family's destruction is that Wigglesworth exults in the breaking, identifying gleefully and self-confidently with Christ the Judge, while Mrs. Rowlandson doubts her own sanctity, sympathizes with victims and devils, and acknowledges a sharing of responsibility with the home-destroying Indian.

Once in the wilderness condition, the captive is figuratively in hell. Like the "natural man" in Edwards's sermon, whose piteous and hopeless situation moved his audience to identification and terror, the captive speaks to his reader directly from hell. He is surrounded by men who appear to be devils. He is tempted to share in their sinful orgies. He has an acute sense of his own depravity, his inability to resist temptations and compulsions toward uncleanness. Living beings demonstrate before his eyes his human bondage to sin. Witnessing this picture, whether as actual captive or as imaginative reader, the unconverted man or woman feels the pain of separation from all the good things of God's world and heaven. For the captive, the

[19]*Pilgrim's Progress*, p. 11.

wilderness is the physical type of metaphysical hell. For the reader, the wilderness is a vivid analogue of the condition of his own inner being—a paradigm of his mind and soul in which his sins, hidden under hopes and rationalizations, are suddenly made manifest.

The throes of the soul's regeneration begin with a sense of separation, a perception of the distance one has fallen from grace. With this comes the perception of sin and sinfulness as a total environment, a world like hell, in which one breathes, gnaws, drinks one's own spiritual filthiness. Thus, for Mrs. Rowlandson and her reader, time is marked not in temporal days but in "Removes," spatial and spiritual movements away from civilized light into Indian darkness. The nadir of her spiritual and physical "progress" in captivity finds her at "twenty removes" from civilization and Christianity. Her choice of the word *removes* and her use of this method of marking the passage of time reinforce the impression of captivity as an all-environing experience, a world in microcosm, complete even to having its own peculiar time-space relationships.

Mrs. Rowlandson swiftly identifies the wilderness of her exile with hell in a vivid portrayal of an Indian bacchanal. Having glutted their appetite for slaughter, the Indians now begin killing and roasting a profusion of domestic beasts:

> Oh the roaring, and singing, and danceing, and yelling of those black creatures in the night, which made the place a lively resemblance of hell. And as miserable was the wast[e] that was there made, of Horses, Cattle, Sheep, Swine, Calves, Lambs, Roasting Pigs, and Fowl...some roasting, some lying and burning, and some boyling to feed our merciless enemies.[20]

This gluttony takes on an added significance as the tale of captivity continues, for hunger is the pervasive misery that dominates the lives of captives and Indians alike, driving them to all manner of sins, making Mrs. Rowlandson eventually their sister in guilt.

At first her restraint is strong in the face of temptation. She is brought before King Philip himself, who "bade me come in and sit down, and asked me whether I would smoke." Mrs. Rowland-

[20]*Soveraignty and Goodness of God*, p. 121.

son here reassures her reader that this, although "a usual com-
pliment nowadays amongst Saints and Sinners" in Christian
Boston, is a temptation the poor Indian captive can still resist:
"For though I had formerly used Tobacco, yet I had left it ever
since I was first taken. It seems to be a Bait, the Devil lays to make
men lose their precious time."[21] But, though she will not partake of the Indian's ceremonial herb, hunger forces her to share
the Indian's meat. She roundly condemns Indians who steal her
ration. ... Yet toward the end of her ordeal she is so far weakened
as to be guilty of the same crime toward two captive children:

> I went to another Wigwam, where they were boyling Corn and
> Beans, which was a lovely sight to see, but I could not get a taste
> thereof. Then I went to another Wigwam where there were two of
> the English Children; the Squaw was boyling Horses feet; then she
> cut me off a piece, and gave one of the English Children a piece
> also. Being very hungry I had quickly eaten up mine, but the
> child could not bite it, it was so tough and sinewy, but lay sucking,
> gnawing, chewing and slabbering of it in the mouth and hand,
> then I took it of the Child and eat it myself, and it was savoury to
> my taste. Then I may say as Job, chapter vi. 7. *The things that my
> soul refused to touch are as my sorrowful meat.*[22]

She feels herself metamorphosed into a beast, a wilderness thing.
The experience of captivity thus leads her to the perception of
her own fallen, debased, even beastlike condition, her absolute
dependence on God, her weakness in the face of sin, and the
precarious nature of all human conditions. "I have seen the extreme vanity of this world," she declares.[23] With this awakening
and the arrival of a ransom, the chastened victim is returned to
society and restored to her family and the community of Saints.

In the formula that was to become conventional, the return and
restoration of the God-wounded sinner marks the conclusion of
the captivity. The captive is not initiated into an entirely new way
of life; rather, he is restored to his old life with newly opened
eyes. Thus the pain and anxiety of the captive—particularly his
traumatic alienation from family and people—are partially re-

[21] Ibid., p. 134.
[22] Ibid., p. 149.
[23] Ibid., pp. 166-67.

solved. And in the symbolic resolution of the captive's trial, the community's anxieties about emigration and about the conflict between generations are likewise resolved. Yet the captive, like the regenerate convert, has experienced a thing that his fellows have not, and his return to their presence is therefore not complete; for part of him always senses, always relives the moment of insight. He has perceived that life is lived on the brink of an abyss, and this perception stays with him as an acute and continuing anxiety for the state of his soul and the wrath of God's judgment on sinful people. Edwards again provides the perfect expression of this sense of isolation and perpetual peril:

> O sinner! Consider the fearful danger you are in: it is a great furnace of wrath, a wide and bottomless pit, full of the fire of wrath, that you are held over in the hand of that God, whose wrath is provoked and incensed as much against you, as against many of the damned in hell. You hang by a slender thread, with the flames of divine wrath flashing about it, and ready every moment to singe it and burn it asunder; and you have no interest in any Mediator, and nothing to lay hold of to save yourself, nothing of your own, nothing that you have ever done, nothing that you can do, to induce God to spare you one moment.[24]

The Puritans believed that the sense of grace, of acceptance by God the Father, grew directly out of such moments of intense fear, anxiety, and loneliness. They therefore hoped that the experience of grace, the sensible apprehension of God by the soul in conversion, would end this feeling of anxious isolation. Thus the saved man in Wigglesworth's "Day of Doom" finds a new home in Christ's bosom, and the Puritan fathers hoped to find in the New World a true "home" for their families and their faith. Hence arises the movement of the captivity myth through images of exile to images of reconciliation and abiding rest. But Mrs. Rowlandson's experiences have marked her and left her spiritually alienated from her family. The restoration to the paternal bosom is incomplete. She has seen through the veil that covers the face of God and cannot lose the sorrowful, necessary knowledge in the bosom of her restored family and church:

[24]"Sinners in the Hands of an Angry God," p. 165.

> I can remember a time, when I used to sleep quietly without work-
> ings in my thoughts, whole nights together, but now it is other
> wayes with me. When all are fast about me, and no eye open, but his
> who ever waketh, my thoughts are upon things past, upon the
> awful dispensation of the Lord towards us...through so many
> difficulties,...returning us to safety.... I remember in the night
> season, how the other day I was in the midst of thousands of
> enemies, and nothing but death before me: It was then hard work
> to perswade myself, that ever I should be satisfied with bread
> again. But now we are fed with the finest of Wheat and, as I may
> say, with honey out of the rock.[25]

Nor is Mrs. Rowlandson's alienation only emotional. She has
acquired a view of the war that is at odds with the orthodox histories. She interrupts her account of her rescue to criticize the
policies and behavior of the colonial governments and their
neglect of the frontier. Moreover, she has found that the Indians
are truly her kindred in spirit: they are as much capable of charity
as her own people, and she is as capable of doing evil as they.
The text chosen for her narrative, "Out of the eater has come
forth meat," thus has an ironic significance. She has partaken of
the Indians' world, their bread and wine; she has devoured it as
it would have devoured her. She became (for a while) Indian-
like in her behavior; she gained insight into the Indian heart
and lived intimately with the Indians. This partaking of the
"Black Eucharist" was an inevitable part of her experience. Her
resistance to adopting the Indians' ways has prevented her captivity from becoming a complete initiation into the American
wilderness, as well as an experience of alienation from the security of the past. The Boone myth and other later myths would
express the growing consciousness of an American national identity in terms of a partial acceptance of initiation into the Indian's
world, but for the Puritan this was impossible. Even the meta-
morphosis of a white man into an animal later became an acceptable part of the Puritan myth, but not the loss of one's identity as
English and Christian.

Mrs. Rowlandson's literary success during her lifetime and her
more enduring success as the originator of a major stream in the
American mythology were not due to artistic skill. She was a

[25]*Soveraignty and Goodness of God,* p. 166.

sensitive woman, a careful observer of both external circumstances and conditions of the mind or soul, reasonably well read
in Scripture, and capable of writing clear, vigorous, often moving
narrative prose. But the power of her narrative to touch and
illuminate the deeper structures of Puritan thought, feeling, and
tradition is due less to conscious art than to the fact that her
experience, training, and state of mind were accurate reflections
of the experience and character of her culture as a whole. Her
greater degree of natural sensitivity and her experience as a captive made her more capable than her fellows of discovering and
revealing the character of her soul, but the soul she revealed
mirrored the aspirations and anxieties of Puritan America.

The Garden of the Chattel:
Robert Beverley and William Byrd II

by Lewis P. Simpson

The Virginians of the post-Virginia Company era made a different kind of response to modern history from that of the New Englanders, defining their mission not as an errand into a howling wilderness, in the midst of which as God's regenerate band they would make a pleasure garden for Him, but as an errand into an open, prelapsarian, self-yielding paradise, where they would be made regenerate by entering into a redemptive relationship with a new and abounding earth. The vision of Virginia as a paradise, in contrast to a wilderness, as a matter of fact, appears in the literature of the Virginia Company days, notably in the writings of Captain John Smith. But the appearance of such a vision in a developed form does not occur until nearly a century later, when it becomes a major aspect of Robert Beverley's remarkable work, *The History and Present State of Virginia.*

Published in London in 1705, this book offers an ecstatic and sensuous vision of the paradisical garden of Virginia. All of the second part—"Of the NATURAL *Product and Conveniencies* of VIRGINIA; In ITS Unimprov'd STATE, before the *English* went thither"—is virtually a fertility hymn in praise of Virginia's waters and fish, and of its soils, native fruits, herbs, and grains. When Beverley comes to consider "the Husbandry and Improvements of the Country"—that is, the development of the Virginian plantations—he is also at times in a near ecstasy. Tending not so much to juxtapose as to blend the delights of the natural garden and the plantation garden, he finds a memorable symbol in the summer house of Colonel William Byrd I:

> Have you pleasures in a Garden? All things thrive in it, most surpriseingly [sic]; you can't walk by a Bed of Flowers, but besides the entertainment of their Beauty, your Eyes will be saluted with the charming colours of the Humming Bird, which revels among the Flowers, and licks off the Dew and Honey from their tender Leaves, on which it only feeds. Its size is not half so large as an *English* Wren, and its colour is a glorious shining mixture of Scarlet, Green, and Gold. Colonel Byrd, in his Garden, which is the finest in that Country, has a Summer-House set round with the *Indian* Honey-Suckle, which all the summer is continually full of sweet Flowers, in which these Birds delight exceedingly. Upon these Flowers, I have seen ten or a dozen of these beautiful Creatures together, which sported about me so familiarly, that with their little Wings they often fann'd my Face.[1]

In his desire to make a complete harmony of Virginia as a natural and an improved garden—"a paradise improved"—Beverley offers a poetic evocation of a plantation summer house and almost ignores the concrete details of the life on the plantation. But in Beverley's poetic evocation we have the origin of the plantation in the literary imagination as the fruition of the errand into paradise. The glimpse of a planter like a Beverley or a Byrd seated pleasantly amid the honeysuckle and the humming-birds in that faraway summer, foreshadows the evocation in literary imagining of a pastoral plantation situated in a timeless "Old South," a secure world redeemed from the ravages of history, a place of pastoral independence and pastoral permanence. To the incomplete scene we have only to add the plantation mansion and the planter, who has in hand a well-worn copy of Virgil, and within a supervisory distance a group of Negro slaves amiably at work in a tobacco field.

At the time Beverley wrote his "honest Account of the an-

---

[1]*The History and Present State of Virginia*, ed. Louis B. Wright (Chapel Hill: University of North Carolina Press, 1947), pp. 298-99. Cf. Leo Marx, *The Machine in the Garden: Technology and the Pastoral Ideal in America* (New York: Oxford University Press, 1964), pp. 75-88.

cientest, as well as the most profitable Colony, depending on the Crown of *England*,"[2] the significance of the individual plantation as a symbol of independent dominion had only begun to emerge. The translation of paradise into the "paradise improved" desired by Beverley occurs specifically in the imagination of William Byrd II, or as he is best known, William Byrd of Westover. It can, in fact, be documented in one letter Byrd wrote in 1726 to an old acquaintance, the Earl of Orrery. Byrd, lately returned from what proved to be his last journey to the mother country, explains the benefits of life in Virginia, if with a poignant reservation:

> Besides the advantage of a pure air, we abound in all kinds of provisions without expense (I mean we who have plantations). I have a large family of my own, and my doors are open to everybody, yet I have no bills to pay, and half-a-crown will rest undisturbed in my pockets for many moons together. Like one of the patriarchs, I have my flock and herds, my bondmen and bondwomen, and every sort of trade amongst my own servants, so that I live in a kind of independence on everyone but Providence. However, though this sort of life is without expense, yet it is attended with a great deal of trouble. I must take care to keep all my people to their duty, to set all the springs in motion, and to make everyone draw his equal share to carry the machine forward. But then 'tis an amusement in this silent country and a continual exercise of our patience and economy. Another thing, My Lord, that recommends this country very much: we sit securely under our vines and our fig trees without any danger of our property. We have neither public robbers nor private, which your Lordship will think very strange when we have often needy governors and pilfering convicts sent amongst us. ... Thus, My Lord we are very happy in our Canaans if we could but forget the onions and fleshpots of Egypt.[3]

In William Byrd's letter to Lord Orrery, we note, the fulfillment of the errand into paradise is realized exclusively in terms of the plantation society of Virginia. This society, if in ironic playfulness, is identified with the promised land of the archetypal Exodus: the plantations of Virginia are New Canaans, which are a powerful and complete salvation from a land in which

[2]Beverley, *History of Virginia*, p. 5.

[3]Pierre Marambaud, *William Byrd of Westover, 1674-1744* (Charlottesville: University Press of Virginia, 1971), pp. 146-47.

the allurements of evil have been a bondage. But the most significant feature of Byrd's vision is that it identifies the new way of life gained by the errand into paradise with the plantation master's supervision of "bondmen and bondwomen." He may refer both to indentured servants and to slaves; but we can assume Byrd refers mostly to his increasing force of chattel slaves. Such an assumption is supported by the preoccupation with slavery that is found elsewhere in his letters and in other writings during the last third of Byrd's career. This was the age of a rapid growth in the number of slaves imported into Virginia in answer to the increasing need for cheap labor in the production of tobacco which could be priced low enough to compete effectively in the European markets. The large importation of slaves was not a considered act. It was an expediency brought about by unpredictable changes in an international market.

In evaluating the result of this, and perhaps without necessarily indicating approval of other general theses of his noted book on slavery in America, I can appeal to the authority of Stanley Elkins. He makes, I think, a most telling point about the introduction of African chattel slavery into the colonial South:

> There was nothing "natural" about it; it had no necessary connection with either tropical climate or tropical crops: in Virginia and Maryland, where the institution first appeared and flourished, the climate was hardly tropical, and the staple crop—tobacco— might have grown as far north as Canada. It had nothing to do with characteristics which might have made the Negro peculiarly suited either to slavery or the labor of tobacco culture. Slavery in past ages had been limited to no particular race, and the earliest planters of colonial Virginia appear to have preferred a laboring force of white servants from England, Scotland, and Ireland, rather than of blacks from Africa. Nor was it a matter of common-law precedent; for the British colonists who settled in areas eventually to be included in the United States brought with them no legal categories comparable to that of "slave," as the term would be understood by the end of the seventeenth century. "Slavery," considered in the abstract as servile bondage, had existed elsewhere for centuries; indeed, the native of Africa had known it intimately. Yet nothing was inherent, even in the fact of *Negro* slavery, which should compel it to take the form that it took in North America. Negro slavery flourished in Latin America at that same period, but

there the system was strikingly different. In certain altogether crucial respects slavery as we know it was not imported from elsewhere but was created in America—fashioned on the spot by Englishmen in whose traditions such an institution had no part. American slavery was unique, in the sense that, for symmetry and precision of outline, nothing like it had ever previously been seen.[4]

When the colonial Virginians expedientially committed themselves—and the South—to African slavery, they instigated an opposition to modern history that they could not institutionalize within the framework of their civilizational tradition. Out of expediency, in other words, they bound themselves to an action that in effect transcended reaction, for it transcended the continuity of their history. But they of course did not realize this. The imagination always works to accommodate novelty to received patterns. With its eruption into the colonial South, beginning in the third decade of the eighteenth century, chattel slavery asked to be taken into the general myth of the New World as a reactionary and redemptive garden; or, more specifically speaking, it demanded to be incorporated in the myth of the South as an errand into paradise. We can see the process commencing in Byrd's letter to Orrery. At this stage it seems to be comparatively simple and painless, involving no more than the creation—out of a stock of images familiar to the colonial mind— of an image of the slave society as a patriarchal garden. But as the population of "Ethiopians" continued to increase, Byrd became conscious of the difficulty of assuming the assimilation of slavery to the pastoral ideal. Slaves, he said in a letter to the Earl of Egmont in 1736, "blow up the pride and ruin the industry of our white people, who, seeing a rank of poor creatures below them, detest work for fear it should make them look like slaves. Then that poverty, which will ever attend upon idleness, disposes them as much to pilfer as it does the Portuguese, who account it much more like a gentleman to steal than to dirty their hands with labor of any kind." Byrd feared too that masters faced with large numbers of slaves would be required to ride them with "a taut rein." This necessity could be "terrible to a good-natured

[4]*Slavery: A Problem in American Institutional and Intellectual Life* (Chicago: University of Chicago Press, 1968), pp. 37-38.

man, who must submit to be either a fool or a fury." The most fearful prospect Byrd envisioned was a servile war instituted by the "descendants of Ham" under the leadership of some "man of desperate courage." This possibility moved him to think that the British Parliament ought to consider the abolition of slavery, or at least a ban on the further importation of black chattels into the colonies.[5] Such promptings of fear did not become overriding considerations with Byrd. He belonged to a world in which slavery had become a necessity—a world in which necessity would be more and more equated with historical destiny. Accepting the developing actuality of his society—the centrality of chattel slavery in his world—Byrd continued to explore the image of the patriarchical garden. His most significant evocation of it, besides the letter to Orrery, may well be a letter ten years later to Peter Beckford of Jamaica. Byrd was interested in having Beckford, a man of great wealth, as a visitor at Westover, probably hoping to sell him land.

> I had the honor to pay you my Respects in June last & to send you as perfect a description of my seat of Westover as truth would permit me. I represented it honestly as it is & us'd not the french liberty of dressing it up as it ought to be. But since my last I have got a person to make a draught of it which perhaps will appear a little rough, but if it should not be found according to Art, it will make amends by being according to truth. Many particulars are left out which could not conveniently be crowded in to so small a Plan, but the Garden & chief of the Buildings are comprehended. I wish all my Heart it may tempt you at least to make us a visit in the Spring in order to see it. But if the Torrid Zone be still your choice & you should resolve to lay your Bones where you first drew your Breath, be so good as to honour this Country with one of your sons, of which I hear you are blest with several, you may make a Prince of Him for less money here than you can make Him a Private Gentleman in England. We live here in Health & in Plenty, in Innocense & Security, fearing no Enemy from Abroad or Robbers at home. Our Government too, is so happily constituted that a Governour must first outwit us before he can oppress us, and if ever he squeeze money out of us he must first take care to deserve it. Our negroes are not so numerous or so enterprizeing

[5]Marambaud, *William Byrd*, pp. 171-72.

as to give us any apprehension or uneasiness nor indeed is their Labour any other than Gardening & less by far that what the poor People undergo in other countrys. Nor are any crueltys exercized upon them, unless by great accident they happen to fall into the hands of a Brute, who always passes here for a monster. We all lye securely with our Doors unbarred & can travel the whole country without either arms or Guard, and all this not for want of money or Rogues, but because we have no great cities to shelter the Thief or Pawn-Brokers to receive what he steals.[6]

The most interesting aspect of Byrd's letter to Beckford is the definition of the role of the chattel slave in the idealized plantation garden. The blacks are not numerous (when in fact their numbers were steadily increasing). Save for gross exception, they are never treated harshly. They are the gardeners in the garden. If Byrd's recognition that in the imagination of the plantation garden the slave, not the master, must be accorded the figurative role of the gardener appears to be hardly more than incidental, it is one of his most important meanings in the literary history of the South. Byrd defined poetically an anxiety that was beginning to haunt the Virginia masters. It was an anxiety about laborers in the earth that was not present in countries where the "poor people" toiled on the land in their role as a peasantry. It was not necessary to think of these people; they did not truly exist except as a part of the immemorial landscape. They were part and parcel of the lord's possession, both actually and imaginatively, of the land. But chattel slaves were property in themselves. The lord of a chattel slave had property in land and property in the slave. The two possessions were not identical but separate. Not only did the master know this but the slave knew it. Thus arose a fear compounded by the racial dimension of slavery but not produced by it: the fear of slavery as being not simply a threat to the social order but of its being a subversion of the very source of order—that is, the mind and imagination.

For subtly attached to the metaphor of the plantation as a pastoral social order, in which the chattel is the gardener, is a more complex metaphorical notion—one that derives primarily from the Western (and not the Hebraic) pastoral. This is the idea of the plantation as a homeland of the life of the mind. In the

[6]*Virginia Magazine of History and Biography*, IX (January 1902), 234-35.

letter to Lord Orrery, Byrd's vision of the plantation as a pastoral community fundamentally derives from the Virgilian imagination of a pastoral world which is a symbolic place of the literary mind and spirit. In the *Eclogues* Virgil established Arcadia in the literary imagination as a dominion of the life of the literary mind. Arcadia, together with the urban image of the mind (and often in contrast to it) became a primary symbol of literary community in the Renaissance, presenting the image of the philosopher and/ or the poet—i.e., the man of letters—in rural retirement, living autonomously in the mind, and yet in an isolation meaningful only because it is in relation to the community of men of letters and learning. The library in the garden—e.g., Pope's grotto at Twickenham—is a pastoral image supporting the concept of the independent, secular, eighteenth-century mind following the pursuits of literature and knowledge. Byrd among his thirty-six hundred books at Westover, engaged in his correspondence with other men of letters, is a figure in the community of the eighteenth-century mind. The pastoral prose may seem superficial in Byrd, as in a letter to John Boyle in 1726: "We that are banished from these polite pleasures [in London] are forced to take up with rural entertainment. A library, a garden, a grove, and a purling stream are the innocent scenes that divert our leisure."[7] But in the context of the adaptation of the pastoral convention in America, William Byrd of Westover is the first full-fledged embodiment of a singular figure in American and, you might say, in Western literature: the patriarch-philosophe—the slave master and man of letters—of the Southern plantation world.

---

[7]Marambaud, *William Byrd*, p. 147.

Jonathan Edwards and Typology

by Ursula Brumm

Jonathan Edwards, the "last" and most important of the American Puritans, has enjoyed a remarkable renaissance in recent years. He has been acknowledged as a forerunner of Transcendentalism and as a force that helped shape American literature.[1] He is even being read, for instance, in the volume of selections carefully edited by Clarence H. Faust and Thomas H. Johnson, who have gathered the pieces of most interest to the modern reader.[2] These selections reveal Edwards as a theoretician in natural science, as a psychologist, as a philosopher, and in the case of the famous sermon "Sinners in the Hands of an Angry God," also as a theologian. What they do not reveal is the extent to which Edwards was a typologist and that his theory of the coherence and the processes of the world was derived from typology. His typologically dominated works have most likely been left aside on purpose as being too abstruse and tedious for the modern reader. Among them we may count many if not almost all of his sermons, his exegesis ("Passages of Scripture"), and the historical work *Thoughts on the Revival of Religion in New England.*

[1]Perry Miller, *Jonathan Edwards* (New York, 1949). The modernity of Edwards alleged there is criticized by Vincent Thomas in "The Modernity of Jonathan Edwards," NEQ, XXV (1952).

[2]*Jonathan Edwards, Representative Selections,* with Introduction, Bibliography and Notes, by Clarence H. Faust and Thomas H. Johnson (American Book Company, 1935).

God Glorified in the Work of Redemption is world history seen theologically from the fall of Adam to the end of the world.[3] But the *Revival of Religion in New England* is contemporary history. It deals with the events that entered history as the "Great Awakening," in which Edwards was a direct participant. This revival movement, which did produce some rather dubious and hysterical outbreaks, lay open to attack from the clergy itself, against whom Edwards defended it with a passion born of conviction. The only portion of his defense that is read today is his letter to a colleague, Benjamin Colman, the "Narrative of Surprising Conversions,"[4] and not the more fundamental and comprehensive work *Thoughts on the Revival of Religion in New England.*[5] Only in this treatise do we discover why Edwards took part heart and soul in the events of the Great Awakening. He regarded this movement with overwhelming expectations in the belief that it marked the beginning of the millennium.

Edwards' attitude toward the revival is connected with his view of religious affections. To these he devoted several sermons some years later, which he subsequently worked up into a treatise. Affections are powers of the human soul bound up with the will and located primarily in the heart. Though some uses of the affections are false and deceptive, and others are connected up with man's animal nature, these affections are nonetheless the vital force of religion. This allows Edwards to account for the abuses of the revival movement as regrettable but understandable (and scarcely avoidable) by-products of an enormous activation of the religious powers in man. He does not doubt for a moment that the revival is God's work (p. 310):

> There are many things in the word of God, that show that when God remarkably appears in any great work for his church, and against his enemies, it is a most dangerous thing, and highly provoking to God, to be slow and backward to acknowledge and honor God in the work, and to lie still and not to put to a helping hand.

[3] I cannot share Perry Miller's opinion (*Jonathan Edwards*, p. 311) that this is "a pioneer work in American historiography."

[4] The original letter is dated May 30, 1735; an expanded version dated November 6, 1736, was published in London in 1737 under the title "A Faithful Narrative of the Surprising Work of God...."

[5] *The Works of President Edwards* (New York and London, 1849), Vol. III, p. 274 ff.

For the clergy it is almost criminal negligence to stand by idly, because whatever lies behind the numerous conversions and the overall revival of religious life must be something special. Edwards thinks that it is the preparation for the millennium: "It is not unlikely that this work of God's Spirit, that is so extraordinary and wonderful, is the dawning, or at least, a prelude of that glorious work of God, so often foretold in Scripture, which in the progress and issue of it shall renew the world of mankind" (p. 313).

There is something remarkable in the discovery of an acute eighteenth-century mind believing that the worldwide revival proclaimed by God has already begun.[6] It is equally remarkable in the context of American intellectual history to find this belief—already anachronistic at that time—bound up with a future-oriented belief in the American nation as the chosen land. Edwards sets out to show why God wants this project begun in America. It is not only "in some measure to balance things," since Europe and Asia have already had their share of great religious events, but also because America is especially deserving of it.

> The other continent hath slain Christ, and has from age to age shed the blood of the saints and martyrs of Jesus, and has often been as it were deluged with the church's blood: God has therefore probably reserved the honor of building the glorious temple to the daughter, that has not shed so much blood, when those times of the peace, and prosperity, and glory of the church shall commence, that were typified by the reign of Solomon.[7]

Long before the separation from Europe, we encounter here a purely religious rather than a political version of the view that Europe is corrupt and guilty of shedding blood, whereas America is peace-loving, happy, and innocent.

Edwards finds the proof of this incipient revival of mankind in typical prefigurations.

---

[6]The rationalist faction in the New England clergy rejected this belief. Edwards' opponent, Charles Chauncey, who objected to Edwards' "preaching of terror," advanced some criticism of Edwards' *Revival of Religion* in his *Seasonable Thoughts on the State of Religion in New England* (Boston, 1743). *Cf. Jonathan Edwards, Representative Selections*, p. xxi.

[7]*The Works of President Edwards*, Vol. II, p. 314. "The other continent" refers as the context shows to "the old world" Asia and Europe together.

Most of the great temporal deliverances that were wrought for
Israel of old, as divines and expositors observe, were typical of the
great spiritual works of God for the salvation of men's souls, and the
deliverance and prosperity of his church, in the days of the gospel;
and especially did they represent that greatest of all deliverances
of God's church, and chief of God's works, of actual salvation, that
shall be in the latter days; which as has been observed is above all
others, the appointed time, and proper season of actual redemption
of men's souls.[8]

Edwards finds types for this "actual salvation, that shall be in
the latter days" in Solomon's kingdom, in Isaiah, in the Feast of
Tabernacles, and in many other Old Testament signs. Then he
attempts to prove that these types were coined for America, or
more specifically, for New England. Isaiah's prophecies indicate
that God will perform his final and greatest work for mankind in
the wilderness, because "When God is about to turn the earth
into a Paradise, he does not begin his work where there is some
good growth already, but in a wilderness."[9] The rescue of He-
zekiah and his city from the Assyrians and the turning back of
the sun, which Isaiah tells of at II Kings 20:9 to 11 are types for
the resurrection of Christ and for "the Sun of Righteousness."
From this Edwards infers that:

The Sun of Righteousness has long been going down from east to
west; and probably when the time comes of the church's deliverance
from her enemies, so often typified by the Assyrians, the light will
rise in the west, until it shines through the world, like the sun in its
meridian brightness... And if we may suppose that this glorious
work of God shall begin in any part of America, I think if we consider the circumstances of the settlement of New England, it must
needs appear the most likely of all American colonies, to be the
place whence this work may principally take its rise. And if these
things are so, it gives more abundant reason to hope that what is
now seen in America, and especially in New England, may prove
the dawn of that glorious day: and the very uncommon and wonderful circumstances and events of this work, seem to me strongly
to argue that God intends it as the beginning or forerunner of
something vastly great.[10]

[8]*Ibid.*, p. 319.
[9]*Ibid.*, p. 315.
[10]*Ibid.*, p. 316.

The argument is buttressed and clenched with the type of Babylonian captivity, followed by those of Joshua, the wilderness, and Canaan, which the Puritans had referred to themselves all along:

> When God redeemed his people from their Babylonish captivity, and they rebuilt Jerusalem, it was, as is universally owned, a remarkable type of the spiritual redemption of God's church; and particularly, was an eminent type of the great deliverance of the Christian church from spiritual Babylon, and their rebuilding the spiritual Jerusalem, in the latter days; and therefore they are often spoken of under one by the prophets: and this probably was the main reason that it was so ordered in Providence, and particularly noted in Scripture, that the children of Israel, on that occasion, kept the greatest *feast of tabernacles,* that ever had been kept in Israel, since the days of Joshua, when the people were first settled in Canaan (Neh. VIII. 16, 17); because at that time happened that restoration of Israel, that had the greatest resemblance of that great restoration of the church of God, of which the *feast of tabernacles* was the type, of any that had been since Joshua first brought the people out of the wilderness and settled them in the good land.[11]

Auerbach has explained how the principle of the type contains an expansion into future time. Edwards took this possibility seriously. He jumped to the bold conclusion that the prefigured millennium was beginning here and now. But we must avoid the mistake of regarding this view of history as a mere curiosity or outmoded way of thought. It is the early theological version of that nineteenth-century American view of history which looked rather to the future than to the past. After independence and the founding of the nation this kind of history was written in the conviction that all human events were developing toward the fulfillment of man's aspirations in America. This hope is found at the core of the world views of writers such as Emerson, Whitman, and Mark Twain. It can also be discerned in the ideas of such historians as Bancroft and Motley.

It has to be admitted that this tendency of the late eighteenth- and nineteenth-century American mind to look toward the future was also derived from the optimistic theories of civilization and

[11]*Ibid.*, p. 323.

progress of the French Enlightenment. Condorcet is especially important in this connection. He followed the progress of civilization through the ages to an America that had just achieved independence, which in his view represented the final and highest stage of civilization. However, the theologically-based faith in the future is a preparatory form that preceded rationalist influence. It had nationalistic aspects, and we can trace exactly how it was transmitted to nineteenth-century thinkers.

Thus the characteristic bent of the American mind toward the future is not solely due to the European influence that arrived with the eighteenth-century Enlightenment and was then continuously reinforced by European immigrants fleeing the burdens of history. The nineteenth-century immigrants welcomed the lack of history in their new land, where they wanted to put their economic and political ideals into practice. In the case of the Puritans these practical aspirations were bound up with others stemming from biblical prophecies and the conception of the type.

And so the future-directed ideas of the American colonists received their first literary expression in the typological form of thought. In this tradition we encounter for the first time an ideal, future America, namely, in a work by Timothy Dwight, a grandson of Jonathan Edwards. This late Puritan, who for many years distinguished himself as president of Yale University, was a patriot from the group of Connecticut Wits. In 1785 he composed a lengthy verse epic, *The Conquest of Canaan*. This work is an exhaustive and verbose account of the conquest of Canaan after the Book of Joshua, a topic that seems way off the track for an American patriot at the time of the Revolution. It is in fact nothing other than a typological version of the American battle for independence. For the Calvinist Dwight, the biblical event is a prefiguration and analogy of the liberation of America,[12] and in Bk. X he extols the new Canaan, America, in glowing colors:

> Far o'er yon azure main thy view extend,
> Where seas, and skies, in blue confusion blend,
> Lo, there a mighty realm, by heaven design'd
> The last retreat for poor, oppress'd mankind!

. . . .

[12]"Type" occurs in Dwight in Bk. I, 1. 756 and Bk. V, 1. 195 ff.

> Far from all realms this world imperial lies;
> Seas roll between, and threatening storms arise;
> Alike unmov'd beyond Ambition's pale,
> And the bold pinions of the venturous sail:
> Till circling years the destin'd period bring,
> And a new Moses lifts the daring wing,
> Through trackless seas, an unknown flight explores,
> And hails a new Canaan's promis'd shores.[13]

In our context, which is in the final instance a literary one, Edwards' typological arguments are interesting for another reason. There is a conspicuous feature about the types chosen by Edwards. He almost never relates them to concrete antitypes, and very seldom to Christ as a person. They refer almost exclusively to "spiritual" fulfillments. The liberation from Babylonian captivity is "a remarkable type of the spiritual deliverance of God's church"; in general "Most of the great temporal deliverances that were wrought for the Israel of old [are] typical of the great spiritual works of God for the salvation of men's souls." In the sermon "The Folly of Looking Back in Fleeing Out of Sodom" Edwards explains that the flight from Jerusalem commanded by Jesus "was a type of fleeing out of a state of sin."[14] Similarly, Lot fled in a rush without looking back: "Because his fleeing out of Sodom was designed on purpose to be a type of our fleeing from that state of sin and misery in which we naturally are."[15] Edwards also relates the Feast of Tabernacles as well as many other types to some inner state of man or of the church, an inner state that as a rule has not yet occurred or has only occurred partially and is instead awaited at the end of time. But this facilitates a severance of the type from Christ at one pole of its relation and also in a certain sense from concrete historicity at the other. The more the fulfillment loses its concrete historical character and becomes a spiritual correspondence, the more this mode of interpretation approaches the allegorical, and the more the type approaches the symbol. The antitype, which was once a determinate aspect of Christ's life and works, now changes more and more into an inner meaning. It is related to the concrete type (Feast of Tabernacles,

---

[13]Timothy Dwight, *The Conquest of Canaan* (Hartford, 1785), Bk. X, 1 479 ff.
[14]*The Works of President Edwards*, Vol. IV, p. 403.
[15]*Ibid.*, p. 403 f.

Lot's flight, the escape from Babylon) as a symbolic meaning is related to its symbol. Thus the successors of the Puritans began by using the concept "type" for a sort of symbol similar to the type, and ended up by using it as a synonym for symbol.

Edwards sometimes speaks of a symbol in the positive sense: for instance, in regard to Christ's symbolic act of washing feet. This act cannot be typical in the strict sense because rather than prefiguring Christ it is carried out by him. On this Edwards comments:

> Which action, as it was exceeding wonderful in itself, so it manifestly was symbolical, and represented something else far more important and more wonderful, even that greatest and most wonderful of all things that ever came to pass, which was accomplished the next day in his last sufferings. There were three symbolical representations given of that great event this evening; one in the passover, which Christ now partook of with his disciples; another in the Lord's supper, which he instituted at this time; another in this remarkable action of his washing his disciples' feet. Washing the feet of guests was the office of servants, and one of their meanest offices: and therefore was fitly chosen by our Saviour to represent that great abasement which he was to be the subject of in the form of a servant, in becoming obedient unto death, even that ignominious and accursed death of the cross, that he might cleanse the souls of his disciples from their guilt and spiritual pollution.[16]

Just as in his interpretation of the type, Edwards also ends up in this interpretation of Christ's symbolical action with a state of the soul, namely, regeneration. The subsequent assimilation of type to symbol can be understood on the basis of this case.[17] In certain instances Edwards' sermons approach allegory, as do so many theological presentations. In every case where an abstract theme is the primary matter and biblical or typological correspondences are sought to illustrate it, the function of allegory is fulfilled, at least in theory.

Cotton Mather enlarged the type into parallel and analogy. Edwards weakened the strict theological conception of the type in another way, by making it bear a meaning expressed in imagery.

---

[16]Vol. III, p. 593.
[17]The Passover is also termed symbolical rather than typical.

Thus not long before the end of the Calvinist era, symbolism and allegory lay ready for future hands to take them up.

At his early, sudden death Jonathan Edwards left behind aphorisms that Perry Miller published as *Images or Shadows of Divine Things by Jonathan Edwards*. Some long, some brief, these aphorisms are notes toward a comprehensive system of correspondences that was intended to bring together divine revelation (the Bible), nature, and history in an orderly, hierarchical whole. The basic correspondence postulated by Edwards is between the spiritual world and the natural world, where inferior things are derived from superior:

> 8. Again it is apparent and allowed that there is a great and remarkeable analogy in God's works. There is a wonderfull resemblance in the effects which God produces, and consentaneity in His manner of working in one thing and another throughout all nature. It is very observable in the visible world; therefore it allowed that God does purposely make and order one thing to be in agreeableness and harmony with another. And if so, why should not we suppose that He makes the inferiour in imitation of the superiour, the material of the spiritual, on purpose to have a resemblance and shadow of them? We see that even in the material world, God makes one part of it strangely to agree with another, and why is it not reasonable to suppose He makes the whole as a shadow of the spiritual world?[18]

This system of analogies spreads through all nature, so that the lower forms are imperfect imitations of the higher. Thus the animals are inferior imitations of man, the plants of animals, etc.:

> 59. If there be such an admirable analogy observed by the creatour in His works through the whole system of the natural world, so that one thing seems to be made in imitation of another, and especially the less perfect to be made in imitation of the more perfect, so that the less perfect is as it were a figure or image of the more perfect... Why is it not rational to suppose that the corporeal and visible world should be designedly made and constituted in analogy to

[18]*Images or Shadows of Divine Things,* ed. by Perry Miller (New Haven, 1948), p. 44.

the more spiritual, noble, and real world? It is certainly agreeable to what is apparently the method of God's working.[19]

The instrument Edwards uses to establish these analogies is the concept of the type. From the original correspondence of Old Testament and Christ, which also marks a value increment from prefiguration to fulfillment, from shadow to truth, he transfers it to the enlarged correspondence of natural world and spiritual world. Image 45 gives a biblical text in support of this. But the real reasons for this extension to the cosmos lie in the respect the rising natural sciences were winning for the natural world and its laws.[20] There is an argument that reveals some of the thought behind this in Miscellany No. 362, appended to Image 58:

Indeed, the whole outward creation, which is but the shadows of His being, is so made as to represent spiritual things. It might be demonstrated by the wonderful agreement in thousands of things, much of the same kind as between the types of the Old Testament and their antitypes; and by there being spiritual things being so often and continually compared with them in the word of God. And it is agreeable to God's wisdom that it should be so, that the inferior and shadowy parts of His works should be made to represent those things that are more real and excellent, spiritual and divine, to represent the things that immediately concern Himself and the highest parts of His work. Spiritual things are the crown and glory, the head and soul, the very end, the alpha and omega of all other works... Thus the inferior dispensation of the Gospel was all to shadow forth the highest and most excellent which was its end; thus almost everything that was said or done, that we have recorded in Scripture from Adam to Christ, was typical of Gospel things. Persons were typical persons; their actions were typical actions; the cities were typical cities; the nations of the Jews and other nations were typical nations; their land was a typical land; God's providences towards them were typical providences; their worship was typical worship: their houses were typical houses; their magistrates, typical magistrates; their clothes, typical clothes; and indeed the world was a typical world. And this is God's manner to make in-

[19]*Ibid.*, p. 65. Quite similar ideas will be found in Image 19, p. 46 f.
[20]Perry Miller treats this in his Introduction, mainly on p. 7 ff: "By an unavoidable compulsion, typology was forced to seek for a unity greater than that of the Bible, a unity of History, nature, and theology."

ferior things shadows of the superior and most excellent; outward
things shadows of spiritual; and all other things shadows of those
things that are the end of all things, and the crown of all things.
Thus God glorifies Himself and instructs the minds that He has
made.[21]

Edwards' goal was as ambitious as it is obvious. Deeply influenced by Locke's philosophy, he wanted to make the natural
world (the only one accessible to human comprehension) into the
image of and key to the transcendent world of religion, which
could thus be understood indirectly. Edwards recognized the
danger that the natural laws discovered by Newton could achieve
an authority of their own alongside the authority of divine revelation. Thus they had to be interpreted as types and copies of divine
truths. The book of nature would have to be interpreted by means
of the book of revelation:

The book of Scripture is the interpreter of the book of nature two
ways, viz., by declaring to us those spiritual mysteries that are indeed signified and typified in the constitution of the natural world;
and secondly, in actually making application of the signs and types
in the book of nature as representations of those spiritual mysteries in many instances.[22]

Edwards realized that the only theology that could thrive in
the modern era was one that had a place for nature and cosmic
forces in its scheme.[23] He regarded the law of gravity as a type of
the "spiritual world" in the following manner:

The whole material universe is preserved by gravity or attraction,
or the mutual tendency of all bodies to each other. One part of the
universe is hereby made beneficial to another; the beauty, harmony
and order, regular progress, life, and motion, and in short all the
well-being of the whole frame depends on it. This is a type of love
or charity in the spiritual world.[24]

The modern discovery, the telescope, "Whereby heavenly
objects are brought so much nearer and made so much plainer to
sight and such wonderfull discoveries have been made in the

[21]*Ibid.*, p. 63 f.
[22]Image 156, *ibid.*, p. 109.
[23]*Cf.* Miller on this point, *Images,* p. 18.
[24]Image 79, *ibid.*, p. 79.

heavens, is a type and forerunner of the great increase in the knowledge of heavenly things that shall be in the approaching glorious times of the Christian church."[25]

History recedes into the background compared with these intense efforts to connect nature with the transcendent world. Edwards had little interest in secular history, and church history was already revealed typologically. Thus he envisaged no threat to theology from the side of historiography. He only makes use of two historical events in the service of typology: "the constitution of the Roman polity" (Image 91), and (very extensively) the Roman world conquest, which is interpreted with all its triumphal marches and victory celebrations as a "remarkeable type of Christ's ascension" (Image 81).

From true types or natural "images of divine things" Edwards distinguishes those correspondences in which one natural event expresses another symbolically. In such cases he speaks of "significations":

> There are many things in the constitution of the world that are not properly shadows and images of divine things that yet are significations of them, as children's being born crying is a signification of their being born to sorrow. A man's coming into the world after the same manner as the beasts is a signification of the ignorance and brutishness of man, and his agreement in many things with the beasts.[26]

One may count these "significations," which Edwards obviously regards as an inferior form of relation between earthly things, among the methods of modern symbolism. On the other hand his types are a special sort of symbol with a fixed transcendent meaning. Thus "Hills and mountains [are] types of heaven" (Image 64); "Ravens, that with delight feed on carrion, seem to be remarkeable types of devils, who with delight prey upon the souls of the dead" (Image 61); and "It is a sign that the beautiful variety of the colours of light was designed as a type of the various beauties and graces of the spirit of God that divine and spiritual beauties and excellencies are so often represented in Scripture by beautifull colours" (Image 58). On several occasions we find the

[25]Image 146, *ibid.*, p. 102.
[26]Image 25, *ibid.*, p. 48.

sun and the silkworm employed as types of Christ, in analogy to traditional typology. Finally, Edwards also sets an aspect of the intimate human sphere he obviously considered important in an exalted relation. Images 5, 9, 12, 32, and 56 treat love and marriage as a type of the relation of Christ to the church:

> We are told that marriage is a great mystery, as representing the relation between Christ and the church (Eph. 5, 32). By mystery can be meant nothing but a type of what is spiritual. And if God designed this for a type of what is spiritual, why not many other things in the constitution and ordinary state of human society and the world of mankind?"[27]

These sketches of "Images or Shadows of Divine Things," which occupied Edwards his entire life,[28] are a grandiose attempt (even though we find it futile) to subordinate the entire natural world—cosmos, earth, man, and history—to the power of the divine will by clamping together in a typical relation the natural and supernatural worlds. The type thus becomes a way of regarding natural phenomena as expressions and products of an analogous transcendent world. The transformation of the entire world accessible to human experience into an indicator of a higher religious meaning does of course diminish its reality. Yet this lends it at the same time a superior reality through its harmony with the spiritual world.

The modern reader has some difficulty realizing that Edwards' reasoning is neither abstruse nor naive. Grant him his presuppositions and Edwards develops a consistent and comprehensive world picture; however, it is a typico-transcendent one rather than a mechanico-casual. If the Bible is the word of God, then it follows that its contents establish eternal models. If nature is the creation of God, then it is natural for its phenomena to mirror its origin and for God to express something in them. It is in the form of types, or in the broader sense, of shadows that God projects his rules into the world of nature. They explain the world after the principle of identity rather than that of causality. In Ed-

[27]Image 12, *ibid.*, p. 45.

[28]Differences in handwriting, pens, and inks prove that the entries were made at different times; the editor Perry Miller states "throughout his life," *Images*, p. 1.

wards' theory it is not so much the isolated phenomenon as it is the natural world itself that is a type in relation to the divine world. It is not an isolated act of God's volition to create a particular type; it is rather "God's *manner* to make inferior things shadows of the superior and most excellent" (my italics). But the reference to the "superior and most excellent" automatically does away with the bipolarity and historicity of the original type concept. If natural and historical phenomena represent copies rather than temporally previous models of something superior and spiritual, this means that the antitype here approximates a deeper, purely spiritual meaning instead of being a concrete historical person or event. Edwards' concept of the type approaches that of the secular symbol, from which however the methodical and parallel character of its reference as well as the law that it always contains a transcendent meaning still serve to distinguish it. As the above statement shows, however, the approach to the Platonic doctrine of eternal ideas and their shadowy terrestrial copies occurs as early as Edwards and not first with Emerson. But Edwards actually only lays bare a component that belonged to the notion of the type from the very beginning. A Platonic influence was present at the very inception of the notion of the type by the Fathers.[29]

[29]Erich Auerbach, *Typologische Motive in der mittelalterlichen Literatur,* Schriften und Vorträge des Petrarca-Instituts, II (Cologne, 1953), p. 15.

The *Autobiography* of Benjamin Franklin

by Robert F. Sayre

Each of the three parts of Franklin's *Autobiography* reflects the time and circumstances of its composition. When Franklin wrote the first portion while visiting the Shipleys in Hampshire, he liked England. He was enjoying a welcome period of relief from his official duties, and he assumed the role of a retired country gentleman giving a private account of his unusual and adventurous history. This is certainly the character taken in the opening.

> Dear Son,
> I have ever had a Pleasure in obtaining any little Anecdotes of my Ancestors. You may remember the Enquiries I made among the Remains of my Relations when you were with me in England; and the Journey I took for that purpose. Now imagining it may be equally agreeable to you to know the Circumstances of *my* Life, many of which you are yet unacquainted with; and expecting a Weeks uninterrupted Leisure in my present Country Retirement, I sit down to write them for you.[1]

As Franklin wrote, this piece began to take the shape of a short picaresque novel. It has the young Benjamin Franklin as a hero; and the themes are his ambition to be in business for himself, his education in writing, his inner struggle over religious questions,

[1][*Benjamin Franklin's Memoirs: Parallel Text Edition,* ed. Max Farrand (Berkeley and Los Angeles, 1949), p. 2. All quotations from the *Autobiography* are from the version of the original manuscript in this volume. Succeeding references will be in parentheses.— Ed.]

and his uneven progress toward marriage. He is a bright youth, but a proud one, and his pride and impatience to succeed make him incompatible with his older brother and vulnerable to the praise and promises of other men. Men like Governor Keith of Pennsylvania, the printers Samuel Keimer and Andrew Bradford, Franklin's friend James Ralph, and the merchant Mr. Denham appear in several spots, and Franklin the writer manipulates their entrances in order to give the story suspense and continuity. They also represent various types of villains and friends. Governor Keith is deceitful; Keimer is a braggadocio; Ralph and other young tradesmen and apprentices are indigent, dissipated, incompetent, or slow witted. Mr. Denham, Andrew Hamilton, and Sir William Wyndham are important older men who take notice of the young Franklin and help him along. It is interesting that Franklin describes one such man, Sir Hans Sloane, as having heard of an asbestos purse he had brought from America, come to see him, and "invited me to his House in Bloomsbury Square" (p. 110). In actual fact Franklin had heard that Sloane was "a Lover of Curiosities" and had written offering to sell the purse to him.[2] Either by design or by failure of memory, Sloane is forced into the category of influential men attracted to the young Franklin.

In such ways does the older Franklin publicize his youth and also demonstrate to himself a continuity between the retired gentleman who is writing and the boy and young man who was already receiving attention from men like the indulgent writer. There is a distinct juxtaposition of youth and age in this part of the *Autobiography,* symbolized by the device of writing it as a letter to his son William Franklin. One is led to believe that William was about the age of the young Benjamin, somewhere in his teens or twenties; yet in 1771 he was about forty years old and Governor of New Jersey! The piece was certainly intended for publication, although probably not until after death, and the signs of a letter are literary devices by which the author established his particular relationship to his material.[3] In a sense

[2]*The Papers of Benjamin Franklin,* ed. Leonard W. Labaree and Whitfield J. Bell, Jr. (New Haven, 1959), I, p. 54.

[3]Robert E. Spiller, "Franklin on the Art of Being Human," *Proceedings of the American Philosophical Society* (August 1956), C, p. 313.

Franklin was writing to himself as well as about himself, developing correspondences between the past and the present. It is the changes, the lack of coherence which another sensibility might have found alarming, which Franklin works upon to find dramatic and striking. The famous arrival in Philadelphia, "eating my Roll," is recognized to have enormous emblematic value, and the elder Franklin does all he can to bring out the contrast, "that you may in your Mind compare such unlikely Beginnings with the Figure I have since made there" (p. 60). The writer gives the exact itinerary of the boy's walk through the town, the people he met, the things he did, the places he stopped, and the "Meeting House of the Quakers near the Market...the first House I was in or slept in, in Philadelphia" (p. 64). Franklin was not quite the penniless waif he made himself out to be. He had arrived tired from the boat journey down the Delaware River, he had spent his last pocket money, and he had no change of clothes. But his luggage was coming around from New York by ship. He exaggerated the "unlikely Beginnings" in order to set them off against the adult Franklin. The penniless waif is built up as the opposite yet the origin of the gentleman "expecting a Weeks uninterrupted Leisure in my present Country Retirement."

Continuity between these extremes exists because Franklin discovered it. It is customary to assert that the *Autobiography,* especially this first part of it, owes its structure to Bunyan and Defoe and is a sort of "American Pilgrim's Progress" or American *Robinson Crusoe,*[4] but this is to be too ingenious about supplying sources or to overemphasize Franklin's secularization of religious biography and autobiography. Franklin indeed knew Defoe and Bunyan well, and he refers to both of them in this part of the *Autobiography.* There is, however, a touch of amusement in the elder Franklin's attitude towards Bunyan ("Honest John," "my old favourite Author"), and his interest in Defoe was primarily in the *Essay on Projects,* an interest that shows up chiefly in the second and third parts of the *Autobiography.* The suggestive fea-

---

[4]John Bach MacMaster, *Benjamin Franklin as a Man of Letters* (Boston, 1887), p. 269. Charles L. Sanford, "An American Pilgrim's Progress," *American Quarterly* (Winter, 1954), VI, pp. 297-310; reprinted in *Benjamin Franklin and the American Character,* ed. Charles L. Sanford (Boston, 1955), pp. 64-73.

ture about the supposed debt to these writers lies in the assumption behind it that Franklin's life was a plastic and unformed substance that could be pushed and prodded into whatever mold he chose to put it. This is a rough but valid assumption. It tallies with Franklin's emphasis on the individual's large range of freedom in his own destiny and also with his method of writing about that life—to gather up the materials and see what forms appear.

The distant structural appropriations of *Crusoe* nd *Pilgrim's Progress,* though, are discovered rather than imposed.

The question next arises, how were they discovered? The explanation lies in Franklin's talent for posing and for imagining roles for himself, an aspect of his character that has already been touched upon in his description of his arrival in Philadelphia. It is obvious that the waif was seized and carefully developed after it had once shown itself as a striking illustration of "unlikely Beginnings." It and the other role of the retired gentleman are held together by the professed purpose of writing an imitable tale for the instruction of posterity. The intention is stated in a sentence in the opening paragraph: "Having emerg'd from the Poverty & Obscurity in which I was born & bred, to a State of Affluence & some Degree of Reputation in the World, and having gone so far thro' Life with a considerable Share of Felicity, the conducing Means I made use of, which, with the Blessing of God, so well succeeded, my Posterity may like to know, as they may find some of them suitable to their Situations, & therefore fit to be imitated" (p. 2).

The trouble with this pretense, however, is that not all the deeds are so exemplary; therefore there is another theme of the indulgent older man who "should have no Objection to a Repetition of the same Life from its Beginning, only asking the Advantages Authors have in a second Edition to correct some Faults of the first" (p. 2). This gives him license to remark "errata" such as running from his brother's printing shop, trying to seduce James Ralph's mistress, and not having married Debbie Read earlier. Whimsically building upon his days as both author and printer, he thus gives himself considerable liberty in what he chooses to include. The narrative becomes an adventure in living over the various provisional identities he found for himself until he un-

winds, in the natural course of history, with the modest and ever
so flexible one he used from 1728 until the end of his life, "B.
Franklin, Printer."[5]

It is one demonstration of the number of his provisional identities just to list the various occupations he at some time or another
entertained for himself: clergyman, seaman, tallow chandler and
soap boiler, printer, poet, swimming instructor, and merchant.
It is sententious to call the first part of the *Autobiography* a
bourgeois adaptation of spiritual autobiography, with Franklin's
progress in trade taking the place of knowledge of God, conversion and baptism.[6] Poor Richard's pithy sayings were never so
magisterial as that! It is better to think of Franklin merely trying
on hats until he found that the printer's fit. And even when work
as a printer expressed some of his talents very well (his playfulness, his love of attention, his spirit of adventure and eagerness
for public good), he by no means thought of it as an end of his
endeavor but as a base around which to build further images of
himself: scientist, politician, diplomat.

A nice picture of the freedom Franklin had in the choice of his
occupation appears in his recollection of his father's taking "me
to walk with him, and see Joiners, Bricklayers, Turners, Braziers,
&c. at their Work, that he might observe my Inclination, & en-
deavour to fix it on some Trade or other on Land" (p. 28). (Franklin's father did not approve of his going to sea.) The similar
freedom he felt he had in the development of his habits and personality is demonstrated in his readiness to take up any idea he
met in a book and give it a try. Happening "to meet with a Book,
written by one Tryon, recommending a Vegetable Diet" (p. 38),
he gave up meat and became a vegetarian. After reading some
poems and ballads, he composed two broadside ballads for his

[5]This is, of course, the way he describes himself in the famous epitaph, generally believed to have been composed in 1728. See the discussion of the matter
in *Papers,* ed. Labaree and Bell, I, p. 110. The epitaph is a beautiful illustration
of Franklin's play in assigning identities to himself: "The Body of B. Franklin,
Printer; Like the Cover of an old Book, Its Contents torn out, And stript of its
Lettering and Gilding, Lies here, Food for Worms. But the Work shall not be
wholly lost: For it will, as he believ'd, appear once more, In a new & more perfect Edition, Corrected and amended By the Author. He was born Jan. 6, 1706.
Died   17   ."

[6]*B.F. and the Amer. Char.,* pp. 72-73.

brother's press. And what is most revealing, when he discovered the Socratic method in Greenwood's *English Grammar* and Xenophon's *Memorable Things of Socrates,* he "was charm'd with it, adopted it, dropt my abrupt Contradiction, and positive Argumentation, and *put on* the humble Enquirer & Doubter" (p. 40, italics mine). The poses and masks which Franklin came across in his reading—not only in Bysshe's eighteenth-century translation of Xenophon,[7] but in Addison, Swift, Defoe, Arbuthnot, Gay, Dryden, Pope, and other Augustan satirists[8]—were more than literary ones to be assumed in his scores of hoaxes and pieces of satiric journalism; they were "real" ones to be tried out in life as well. This is evident in Franklin's tireless affection for pranks, for practical jokes, and disguises. Franklin readily slipped into poses in the *Autobiography* because he had lived in a fluid world. His day-to-day identities approached poses.

If no strict and dogmatic religion exactly defined man's role in respect to Heaven and no rigid social structure exactly defined his role on earth, then man's role could be whatever he chose to make it. Franklin was scrupulous in his religious convictions and he was not selfish or single-mindedly accumulative in his worldly activity. The point is that he arrived at both his religious and social philosophies by his own experimentation and intelligence. He recognized his freedom and realized that whatever actions he took were in a dramatic sense, "acts," roles to some degree thrust upon him but also consciously selected and therefore open to whatever interpretations he wished to make of them. The fact that he conducted such a large amount of his business by writing—letters, reports, scientific papers, pamphlets, proposals, propaganda pieces—is interesting in this respect because the printed page was obviously the medium through which he learned many of the gestures and postures of his multiple lives. Still, several lessons from "real life" (as handed on in the *Autobiography*) are to be noticed.

[7]Personal letter from Edwin Wolf, 2nd, Librarian, the Library Company of Philadelphia, December 14, 1960. Mr. Wolf says that "the Library Company in its first order of 1732 asked for a copy of Bysshe's translation and since Franklin helped draw up the list, I had assumed that he was speaking of that version."

[8]Francis Davy, *Benjamin Franklin, Satirist* (University Microfilms, 1958), p. 160.

On his way through New Jersey after having broken his apprenticeship to his brother, Franklin says that he "cut so miserable a Figure" that he was suspected of being "some runaway Servant." As a runaway apprentice he nearly was, but a night later he was not so tired and wretched looking. The innkeeper, his eventual friend, Dr. Brown, "entred into Conversation with me while I took some Refreshment, and finding I had read a little, became very sociable and friendly" (p. 58). Neither the notion of Franklin as the fugitive nor the notion of him as the young travelling scholar expressed the whole truth. If people were to make such hasty judgments, however, it made sense to encourage the more favorable one.

A chase, the iron frame surrounding type, happened to break one evening as Franklin the printer was closing shop. Understandably, he stayed up late to reset the pied pages. From outside his window, nonetheless, he appeared to be working like a man extraordinarily devoted to his trade. Word spread that he was a hard worker and that his house would survive despite the competition of two other printers. The elder Franklin cites this as an instance of the usefulness of the virtue of industry, but from another anecdote it is evident that in actual fact he was not so pedestrian.

> In order to secure my Credit and Character as a Tradesman, I took care not only to be in *Reality* Industrious & frugal, but to avoid all *Appearances* of the Contrary. I drest plainly; I was seen at no Places of idle Diversion; I never went out a-fishing or Shooting; a Book, indeed, sometimes debauch'd me from my Work; but that was seldom, snug, & gave no Scandal: and to show that I was not above my Business, I sometimes brought home the Paper I purchas'd at the Stores, thro' the Streets on a Wheelbarrow (p. 172).

Note the props: the plain dress, the debauching book, the wheelbarrow! Being industrious and frugal was for Franklin a game, a cheerfully entered role. Having noticed that the burghers of Philadelphia (Adams' "true Pennsylvanians…as narrow as a kirk; as shy of other people's narrowness as a Yankee; as self-limited as a Puritan farmer") paid attention to industry and frugality, Franklin quietly went about attracting their attention.

Carl Becker observed that Franklin was never thoroughly submerged in anything he undertook. Everything he did he gave his best to, and most everything he did he did well, but behind the gestures and routines of his participation was always a reserve, a certain ironic sense which took amusement as well as satisfaction from the experience.[9] This was the actor in him; one might almost say the dead-pan comedian in him, and it owed much to the fact that each participation was easily and freely chosen. The man behind the actor was always bigger than the single part. This is a most important fact about Franklin's personality, and it operated in all his achievements on all his many stages. The first section of the *Autobiography* is the story of Franklin's building of his roles —sampling sundry occupations, hoaxes, disguises, and literary masks—and of fitting himself out in the "plain dress" of his first and most lasting public character, flexible and adaptable as it was always to be for him, "Benjamin Franklin of Philadelphia, Printer."

He found it again as he wrote the Twyford part of the *Autobiography*. A step towards the vacationing gentleman who is correcting his "errata," it is also the string that draws everything else into place. Having returned from London and gone into the partnership with Hugh Meredith, he soon organizes his Junto. He and Meredith start a newspaper, the *Pennsylvania Gazette*. Meredith realizes that he was not meant to be a printer, so Franklin gets a loan and takes on the whole business by himself. He writes a pamphlet on *The Nature and Necessity of a Paper Currency* and later receives the contract to print the new money. He adds sidelines of stationery and begins to pay off his loan. His tenants leave after a failure in negotiations for Franklin to marry one of their relations. The whole house left to himself, Franklin marries Debbie Read, who, he says, had first seen him (and laughed at him) when he arrived in Philadelphia eating his roll.

Franklin finds his identity in the first part of the *Autobiography* by reassessing all the provisional roles he played as a young man. The final character of Benjamin Franklin, Printer, is a satisfactory conclusion because it holds within itself both the retired gentleman of Twyford and the penniless waif of "unlikely Beginnings." The work is an amalgam of the man writing and the man written about. The same generalization applies to the two later parts

[9]"Benjamin Franklin," *Dict. Amer. Biog.* (New York, 1943).

composed at Passy in 1784 and in Philadelphia in 1788. What Franklin wrote in France is a most delicate manipulation of his youthful experience to the purposes of the public character he played at Versailles, in the salons of Mmes. Helvetius and Brillon, and in the French press. What he wrote back in Pennsylvania emphasizes his achievements as civic leader and American patriot.

We can begin by noting, however, that the two later parts have one important thing in common: both are accounts of projects. The Passy piece begins where Franklin had left off thirteen years before with the scheme of the Philadelphia Library Company; then, after a few pages on his domestic affairs and church attendance, it launches into the famous "bold and arduous Project of arriving at moral Perfection." The longer Philadelphia memoir is for the most part a chronology of Franklin's many local and colonial projects for a school, hospital, cleaner streets, a better city watch, fire department, militia, and supplies for General Braddock's army. Franklin was fond of conceiving of himself as a projector, and this fondness is one of the most markedly eighteenth-century aspects of his personality. He wrote both satiric projects after the manner of Swift's *Modest Proposal* and De-Foe's *Shortest Way with Dissenters* and non-satiric projects like Defoe's *Essay on Projects*. Simply speaking, the non-satiric are supposed to be taken up and acted upon while the satiric are supposed to rally opposition to the actions the writer urges or assumes will be extended. The important point to realize is that the projector is always wearing a mask, be he the man so anxious for the welfare of Ireland that he cannot understand the inhumanity of raising children for food, or be he the conscientious trades-man who would like to make arrangements for female education or for life insurance.

The mask Franklin wears in describing the "Project of arriving at moral Perfection" is his French one of the *naïf* "Philosophical Quaker," a role both thrust upon him by the acclaim given him on his arrival in France and also cultivated by him in his diplomatic mission, his bagatelles, and even in the modest and ingenuous ways in which he showed his amusement with the role and attempted to deny it.[10] John Adams, who was a severe critic

[10]Alfred Owen Aldridge, *Franklin and His French Contemporaries* (New York, 1957), pp. 59ff.

of many of Franklin's diplomatic maneuvers and, like Abigail Adams, was scandalized by his personal behavior, spoke the truth when he observed that Franklin "was master of that infantine simplicity which the French call *naïveté,* which never fails to charm, in Phaedrus and La Fontaine, from the cradle to the grave."[11]

The disarming quality of the attempt to reach moral perfection was the logic of it. Of the pretentiousness and vanity of such an aim, the young Franklin was sublimely unaware.

> I wish'd to live without committing any Fault at any time; I would conquer all that either Natural Inclination, Custom, or Company might lead me into.

In the next breath the elder Franklin means to disarm the reader as well.

> As I knew, or thought I knew, what was right and wrong, I did not see why I might not *always* do the one and avoid the other (p. 210).

The young man was innocently reasonable, so reasonable that reason deceived him. "But I soon found," it is announced with inimitable understatement, "I had undertaken a Task of more Difficulty than I had imagined." Always doing the right and avoiding the wrong was really rather hard. "While my *Attention was taken up* in guarding against one Fault, I was often surpriz'd by another." Yet reality became a challenge to his diligence instead of a reminder to his modesty; so, adding diligence to his reasonableness, he devised his "Method" for concentrating his attention on one virtue at a time. By maintaining constant watch and subjecting his behavior to minute study, he would still persevere in this most charming madness.

The method was the famous list of thirteen virtues, the little maxims subjoined to each, and the book in which he kept the record of his moral progress. To accept the program didactically as an exemplary exercise in self-improvement or to look upon it cynically as a bumbling tradesman's petty commandments is to miss Franklin's *naïveté,* his cultivated "infantine simplicity." Only Franklin could have conceived it. By comparison, Robinson

[11]*The Works of John Adams,* ed. Charles Francis Adams (Boston, 1856), I, p. 663. Reprinted in *B.F. and the Amer. Char.,* p. 25.

Crusoe's balance sheet of the "Evil" and "Good" in being castaway on his island is primitive, mere arithmetic. Franklin's "moral algebra" is complete with lines in red ink, columns, mottos, dots, abbreviations, headlines. Yet with all these contrivances (or possibly because of them), the method retains its reasonableness and innocence. The intricacy of "arriving at moral Perfection" makes it the most artful of games. Children are absorbed by it.

> I made a little Book in which I allotted a Page for each of the Virtues. I rul'd each Page with red Ink, so as to have seven Columns, one for each Day of the Week, marking each Column with a Letter for the Day. I cross'd these Columns with thirteen red Lines, marking the Beginning of each Line with the first Letter of one of the Virtues, on which Line & in its proper Column I might mark by a little black Spot every Fault I found upon Examination to have been committed respecting that Virtue upon that Day (p. 216).

A sample page is included in the text. Franklin's procedure was "to give a Week's strict Attention to each of the Virtues successively," at the same time keeping account of his performance regarding the others as well. "Thus if in the first Week I could keep my first Line marked T [Temperance] clear of Spots, I suppos'd the Habit of that Virtue so much strengthen'd and its opposite weaken'd, that I might venture extending my Attention to include the next [Silence], and for the following Week keep both Lines clear of Spots" (pp. 218, 220). Proceeding in this way, the young Franklin could go through a complete course in thirteen weeks, or four courses in a year. The beginning of the book was given over to bolstering mottos and prayers; the end contained the "Scheme of Employment for the Twenty-four Hours of a natural Day," which was necessitated by the "Precept of Order." It is a further instance of his *naïveté* that as time went by he "was surpriz'd to find myself so much fuller of Faults than I had imagined." He found, in fact, that the wear and tear of erasing the spots of "old Faults to make room for new Ones in a new Course" was puncturing the pages of his book with holes, so he transferred his tables "to the Ivory Leaves of a Memorandum Book," from which the marks could be wiped away with a wet sponge (p. 226).

Franklin the writer never breaks character in his story of this project or lifts his mask to expose the man beneath. Instead he even accentuates his innocent reasonableness from time to time. "Something that pretended to be Reason was every now and then suggesting to me, that such extream Nicety as I exacted of my self might be a kind of Foppery in Morals, which if it were known would make me ridiculous" (p. 228). He is so reasonable, as well as so diligent, that he does not let this "pretended" voice stop him. He dwells on the great difficulty he confronted with the virtue of "Order," leaving one to wonder that he should have reached "Justice" or "Moderation" more easily. He goes on and attributes to the effect of the "Project" his wealth and well-being and says it had once been his intention to write a great book to be called the *Art of Virtue.* He even shifts briefly into the third person, stating that "my Posterity should be informed, that to this little Artifice, with the Blessing of God, their Ancestor ow'd the constant Felicity of his Life down to his 79th Year in which this is written" (p. 230). Beginning in the rhetoric of understatement, he thus works up to the full-blown language of the *naïf* who has mastered his task and then been mastered by it. He becomes exhortative, rotundly pedagogic. The only way out is by coming back to the subject of "Humility," the last of the thirteen virtues. He says he never succeeded in "acquiring the *Reality* of this Virtue; but I had a good deal with regard to the *Appearance* of it" (p. 234). The concluding paragraph is on pride and humility.

> In reality there is perhaps no one of our natural Passions so hard to subdue as *Pride*. Disguise it, struggle with it, beat it down, stifle it, mortify it as much as one pleases, it is still alive, and will every now and then peep out and show itself. You will see it perhaps often in this History. For even if I could conceive that I had compleatly overcome it, I should probably be proud of my Humility (p. 362).

Thus Franklin collapses his philosopher's hubris in his "Quaker" simplicity. The ten tendencies are beautifully reconciled, the frankly *naïf* young Franklin commencing the project with his scheme to become perfect, the famous elder Franklin carrying the idea along as a worthy endeavor that all men should be interested in, and the sophisticated, consciously *naïf* "Philosophical Quaker" finishing it in a discourse on pride and humility. The experience of fifty years before is thereby examined and recast in the mold of the present. The character of the young man is brought into line with the pose of the older man. His role as rustic philosopher demanded that he should at an early stage in life have entered upon a "bold and arduous Project of arriving at moral Perfection." Naturally, it failed, but the story of that failure was an opportunity to create a plain, reasonable, somewhat comical origin for the sage whose worldliness expressed itself in simplicity.

Franklin's identity in the third part of the *Autobiography* as patriot and civic projector gives it the form of a series of lessons in "doing good." As a series rather than a single story it does not have the interlocking structure of the first section or the roundness of the main part of the second. Perhaps this more literary order was not so available within the material itself. Perhaps the eighty-two-year-old Franklin did not have the artistic control he once had. Yet it is also true that this continued series of experiences does express the multiplicity of his interests and reflect the variety of lives he was leading at the time he wrote it. It bursts with things: fire ladders, dirty streets, smoky lamps, stoves, bags and buckets, wagons, munitions, whiskey, schools, pigs and chickens, bonds and subscriptions, forts. It is also more moralistic than the other parts, and each modern instance is preceded or followed by its wise saw: *"It is hard for an empty sack to stand upright." "He that has once done you a Kindness will be more ready to do you another, than he whom you yourself have obliged." "After getting the first hundred Pound, it is more easy to get the second."* "The best public Measures are therefore seldom *adopted from previous Wisdom,* but *forc'd by the Occasion."*

In context these aphorisms are not banal. On the contrary, they reflect Franklin's uncanny insight as politician and lay psychologist. Back in the midst of Philadelphia, back in the whirl of civic and national contentions, Franklin reinterpreted his earlier undertakings in terms of their present applications. Of all parts of the *Autobiography,* this one is most like a memoir and of most value to the descendants of early American democracy. Franklin's projects strike the modern reader as entirely in the public interest; personal vanities should not have mattered. He became attentive, however, not only to how people *should* feel and respond but also to how they *do.* He allowed others to save their face instead of worrying always about his own. He helped them to go on living by their convictions. Pennsylvania Quakers, for example, were not opposed to "the Defence of the Country...provided they were not requir'd to assist in it" (p. 284). To win support for the public hospital, Franklin devised a system of matching state appropriations and private subscriptions, with the amusing result that members of the Pennyslvania Assembly realized "they might have the Credit of being charitable without the Expence" (p. 310). The trustees of a special meeting house built at the time of Whitefield's revival had to represent each of the many sects in the City. When the same building was taken over by the new Academy, the new governors had to agree to keep open a hall for occasional preachers and "maintain a Free School for the Instruction of poor Children" (p. 298).

When Franklin wrote this part of his *Autobiography* in 1788, the Country was rebuilding from the destruction of the Revolution and in need of new ideas and energies and men with the social and political skill to employ them. Franklin is seeing himself not as the retired gentleman of the first portion of the *Autobiography* or the naïve philosopher of the second, but as the busy Philadelphian. It might be added that this is the only part of the book in which Franklin seems something of an Anglophobe. In the account of General Braddock's campaign, in the offhand remarks about working hours in London, in implications that the Royal Society scorned his scientific experiments, and in criticism of Lord Louden for delaying the ship on which he sailed to England in 1757 — in all these places we know that the Revolution has come between the events and the reminiscences. But this section is most strongly American for its emphasis on *doing* and upon self-realization in public life. It does not present the whole Franklin; it does not present the whole American. But it presents the American Franklin as the writer saw himself at that time. The life has once again been made over in a discovery of the present by means of re-discovering the past.

Whig Sentimentalism

by Kenneth Silverman

Whether verse, cartoons, or public demonstrations, all the forms of Stamp Act protest share two related features: a distinct literary quality—a habit of alluding to *Cato* or Shakespeare while excoriating Bernard or Bute; and a peculiarly vehement emotionalism—a pervasive idiom of groaning, mutilation, and rape that might be called Whig Sentimentalism.

Whig theory reached the colonies through a literary as well as a political tradition. English poets and playwrights contemporary with Trenchard and Gordon adapted Whig ideas to current literary conventions, using the ancient poetic commonplace of rural contentment, for instance, as a counter-image to the rampant bribery and despotic ambition of current city politics. One monument of the Whig poetic tradition was James Thomson's long poem *Liberty,* published in five parts in 1735-36. The meaning Thomson ascribed to liberty is complex, but in its full extent represents progress itself, the means by which civilizations mature and by which mankind as a whole advances to higher levels of consciousness. English drama of the period was also highly politicized. Eighteenth-century theatregoers often saw resemblances to current political events in Shakespeare's history plays and laid political interpretations upon them. Works like *The Beggar's Opera* and *The Clandestine Marriage* portrayed all classes and professions of English society as wallowing in dissoluteness, falsehood, and chicanery, confirming what Trenchard and Gordon charged, while overtly Whiggish plays such as *Gustavus Vasa,*

"Whig Sentimentalism." From Kenneth Silverman. *A Cultural History of the American Revolution* (New York: Thomas Y. Crowell, 1976), pp. 82-86. Copyright © 1976 by Kenneth Silverman. Reprinted by permission of Thomas Y. Crowell.

Douglas, and *The Roman Father*—all of them popular in the colonies—celebrated freedom and patriotism. George Lillo's play *The Christian Hero* contains the phrase "unalienable right," applied to freedom, as well as the phrase "sons of liberty."

By far the most quoted Whig literary work, omnipresent in the Stamp Act protests, was Joseph Addison's *Cato.* The edition of *Cato* which appeared in Boston in 1776 also marked the first publication in America of an English play. Because of his many activities, Cato was portrayed throughout classical and later literature according to ideological vagaries: Both Whigs and Tories claimed him. Addison, however, emphasized the disinterested republican martyr who opposed Roman corruption and committed suicide rather than accept the tyrannical rule of Julius Caesar. First produced in England in 1713 and for the first time in America in 1735, the play applied in virtually every line to the colonial situation in 1765, and later. Its language directly inspired some ringing colonial declarations of purpose, as a few quotations suggest:

> Gods, can a Roman senate long debate
> Which of the two to choose, slavery or death! (II, i)
>
> The gen'rous plan of power delivered down,
> From age to age, by your renowned forefathers,
> (So dearly bought, the price of so much blood)
> O let it never perish in your hands! (III, v)
>
> ...What pity is it
> That we can die but once to serve our country! (IV, iv)

Being what Dr. Johnson called "rather a poem in dialogue than a drama," *Cato* was ideally suited for production by amateurs, who needed only to strike an attitude and declaim; it had a long career in the colonies as a school play. Its politics, too, gave a sanctity to performances that made foes of the theatre cautious. Magistrates in anti-theatre Cambridge were anxious to avoid prosecuting a student production in the early 1770's because, according to one witness, "the prosecution might be misconstrued as if levelled against the sentiments...." The American Company often used the play when under attack by moralists. The play also suggested to the Whig theorists Trenchard and Gordon the title for their essays, *Cato's Letters*. To eighteenth-century readers and theatregoers, the name "Cato" was thus packed with ideological meaning. The career of the historical Roman, the events of Addison's play, and the ideas of the English radicals merged, as Bailyn says, in a powerfully resonant "Catonic" image.

The Stamp Act protests could be described as literary, then, only from a modern perspective. Colonial Whigs could have seen nothing peripheral to politics or merely decorative in comparing November 1, as one newspaper did, "to a description in Addison's Cato," or in publishing on the front page, as another did, a poem entitled "Cato's Soliloquy Imitated." The contributor to the *Boston Gazette* who presented his views on taxation in the form of a version of a scene from *Henry VIII* was doing something which his age understood as politics quite as much as literature. Such pieces should be read not with a mind to the officialese of modern political discourse, but recalling that Benjamin Franklin quoted Homer against the massacre of Indians on the Pennsylvania frontier, that Jefferson wrote on English versification, that James Otis produced not only *The Rights of the British Colonies Asserted and Proved* but also a *Rudiments of Latin Prosody*.

Thus verse and drama of the period are rife with Whig ideas, just as political pamphlets are rife with verse and drama. The Whig literary tradition, fully established after the Glorious Revolution of 1688, became nearly as important a source of political ideas in the colonies as the works of Trenchard and Gordon. Colonists quoted Addison, Thomson, Pope, Milton, and Shakespeare as political authorities hardly less often than they quoted Locke or Montesquieu. Even in nakedly political pamphlets it is often impossible to tell which is the nearer source of ideology.

English poets and playwrights were drawn to Whig theory because they found its moralistic politics congenial to popular moral ideas about benevolence, charity, and the importance of feeling. The connection of commerce with economic relief for the lower classes, for instance, made trade a matter of sentiment and a natural subject for poetry. This fusion of political theory with popular moral sentiment in the Whig literary tradition charged discussions of taxes with powerful emotional associations. The tearful lament of the probate papers,

> ...with many a sigh,
> 'Must we be st--pt,' with tender accent cry:
> 'We who our life and breath, so freely spend,
> 'The fatherless and widow to defend. ...

is not very different in feeling from the poem published in the *Virginia Gazette* in 1767 on the death of an infant:

> WHO, that beheld the lovely boy expire,
> But must have join'd his tears to see
> The weeping mother, and the sobbing sire,
> Involv'd in so much misery?

Whig Sentimentalism made new taxes seem not merely a burden, nor even ministerial extortion, but ultimately a brutalization of those who sigh and are tender, producing the anguished cries at mock funerals, the doleful face of wretched Britannia in Franklin's cartoon. the groaning woe throughout the Stamp Act protests. Similarly, the rural swains who narrated Stamp Act poems or urged a return to the fig leaf or celebrated at Liberty Tree made the tax seem a barbaric affront to the integrity, innocence, and good nature symbolized by pastoral life.

Whig Sentimentalism, then, invested the Stamp Act with emotions belonging to the violation of the most general and highly cherished ideals. None of these ideals was more often invoked by the protestors than that of loving domestic relationships. The verses and demonstrations insistently depict the Stamp Act as primal disloyalty, inflicting pain so unexpected, unwarranted, and unnatural that it can be compared only to a loved parent disowning its child, or a loved child betraying its parent. The comparison underlies pleas to "GEORGE! Parent! King!" as well as William Pitt's famous reminder to the House of Commons, in 1766, that "The Americans are the sons, not the bastards, of England." It mingles and blends with pervasive images of rupture and mutilation—severed snakes, stab wounds, torn limbs, and hacked effigies—that similarly convey a sense of anguish at the cutting of deep bonds. At the August 16 demonstration in Lebanon [Pennsylvania], a female effigy with chained feet, representing America, howled against colonial stamp distributors as prodigal sons:

...thus pleading with her base, unnatural child.—*My Son! remember that I have treated you with the utmost tenderness, and bestow'd on you my highest honours, pity your country, and put not on me these chains;* to which her ungrateful, degenerate son replied, in a label proceeding from his mouth, *Perish my country, so that I get that reward:* upon the utterance of which, such indignant wrath swell'd the bosom of this venerable matron, that her power of speech fail'd....

In another version of disinheritance, England appeared as an aging, increasingly odd parent, jealous that her colonies have developed a distinct personality:

We have an old Mother that peevish is grown,
She snubs us like Children that scarce walk alone;
She forgets we're grown up and have Sense of our own....

Complementing such images of family strain the protests contain many images of new lineage, of better parentage. Many demonstrators claimed a transcendent loyalty, calling themselves sons and daughters of Liberty rather than of England. As mourners drew through Portsmouth the coffin of Liberty marked with the date of the Plymouth landing, the author of *The Times* asked whether the colonists were not obliged primarily to the ideals of the first settlers, and to their own future progeny:

Is it for you their honour to betray?
And give the harvest of their blood away?
Look back with rev'rence, aw'd to just esteem,
Preserve the blessings handed down from them;
If not, look forwards, look with deep despair,
And dread the curses of your beggar'd heir....

As people began identifying themselves more closely with the colonial than with the English past, there emerged the notion of a single origin common to Bostonians and Charlestonians alike, the legend of the forefathers.

The colonists invested their protests with emotions belonging to one other kind of relationship, more subtle and powerful in its appeal than the rest. Feminizing the concept of liberty, they saw themselves as defenders of virtue against an act of rape. "Fair Liberty"—the master symbol of the protests—was a commonplace of Whig literary tradition, although it had an older and continuous history. About 135 B.C. the Roman statesman Graccus created a temple of Liberty in Rome, where he represented Liberty as a Roman matron—*Libertas*—holding a pike topped with a cap. The Romans gave such a cap—*a pileus*—to freed slaves as the sign of their emancipation. The liberty pole and liberty cap became standard accoutrements of Libertas. A coin of Nerva, A.D. 97, shows a female liberty figure and staff, as does a fifth-century coin minted in the reign of Brutus, the executioner of Caesar. Libertas with cap and staff appears widely in Dutch and French prints of the sixteenth century; Addison in *Tatler* no. 161 (1710) gave an allegorical sketch of the Goddess of Liberty, depicting her with a liberty cap, aided by Plenty and Commerce; during the Seven Years' War, Libertas with cap and pike became a very popular image in English prints.

In America, the Libertas image had had wide currency since the 1750's, when the English Whig Thomas Hollis, a benefactor of Harvard College, commissioned a representation for Jonathan Mayhew's *Discourse Concerning Unlimited Submission,* a classic of the American Whig tradition. He first had a gem made depicting a seated Britannia holding pole and cap, beneath which was the date January 30, 1648, marking the execution of Charles I. Hollis then employed the Italian artist Giovanni Battista Cipriani to make a print of the gem, which he sent to Harvard, together with some books on which he had the image stamped. In the last quarter of the eighteenth century, Libertas was an omnipresent image in America, enabling a Son of Liberty to step forward at one mock funeral and groan with the passionate bereavement of a lover, "Oh! *Liberty!* the darling of my soul! glorious *Liberty!* admir'd, ador'd, by all true Britons!—*Liberty* dead!" In defending Libertas, Americans attached to their cause the full force of the sentimental love tradition that defended the guileless purity of daughters and wives against scheming seducers bent on befouling them.

Common Sense and Paine's Republicanism

by Eric Foner

Thomas Paine arrived in Philadelphia on November 30, 1774. Political change was in the air; it dominated discussion in the city's taverns and coffee houses, homes and workshops. Already, the port of Boston had been closed as punishment for the Boston Tea Party of December 1773 and the First Continental Congress had assembled in Philadelphia in the fall of 1774, composed of "the ablest and wealthiest men in America." From New England came the "brace of Adamses"—John and his cousin Samuel—advocates of a policy of resistance to British policies and, many feared, secret friends of American independence. In Congress, Pennsylvania's Joseph Galloway urged a policy of reconciliation, but he was narrowly defeated, and instead Congress in October adopted the Continental Association, an agreement banning all commerce with Britain and the West Indies, and called for the establishment of popularly elected local committees to enforce the prohibition. The Whig leaders of Philadelphia—Dickinson, Thomson and Reed—with their popular base in the artisan community dating from the political conflict of 1770, quickly gained control of the Philadelphia committee, which rapidly replaced the official city government as the real power in local affairs.

Paine arrived in America with the not very revolutionary aim of setting up an academy for the education of young women. But Franklin's letters of introduction soon obtained for him a position as editor of the *Pennsylvania Magazine,* a periodical launched by the publisher and bookseller Robert Aitken. From February to

September 1775, Paine worked as day-to-day editor of the publication and contributed poems and essays of his own.[1]

Like *The Case of the Officers of Excise* of 1772, Paine's early American writings provided an inkling—but only that—of the fully developed political outlook and deep resentment against the inegalitarian structure of English society which Paine would soon express in *Common Sense.* In the very first issue of the *Pennsylvania Magazine* (January 24, 1775), Paine spoke of the "profligacy" and "dissipation of manners" of England and the "virtue" of America, language which had long been familiar to Americans in the writings of the British Commonwealthmen and their American disciples. In another early essay, "Reflections on Titles," Paine wrote, "When I reflect on the pompous titles bestowed on unworthy men, I feel an indignity that instructs me to despise the absurdity." "High sounding names" like *"My Lord"* served only to "overawe the superstitious vulgar," and make them "admire in the great, the vices they would honestly condemn in themselves." Paine also gave voice to the anti-Popery which had permeated the culture of Lewes in England and which was widespread among American Protestants. Criticizing the Quebec Act of 1774, which afforded official recognition to the Catholic faith of the inhabitants of Quebec, he observed, "Popery and French laws in Canada are but a part of that system of despotism which has been prepared for the colonies."

Paine thus seems to have identified himself from the beginning with the fears of many colonials about the intentions of the British government. But on one issue, as the true son of a Quaker, he was critical of Americans as well. "With what consistency, or decency," he asked in a newspaper piece published in March 1775, could the colonists "complain so loudly of attempts to enslave them, while they hold so many hundred thousand in slavery."[2]

Through his connection with the magazine Paine, in 1775, made the acquaintance of the young physician Benjamin Rush,

[1]John C. Miller, *Origins of the American Revolution* (Boston, 1943), 379; Philip S. Foner, ed., *The Complete Writings of Thomas Paine* (2 vols.: New York, 1945), II, 1161; David Freeman Hawke, *Paine* (New York, 1974), chapter 2; Lyon N. Richardson, *A History of Early American Magazines 1741-1789* (New York, 1931), 177-79.

[2]Foner, *Complete Writings,* II, 18, 33, 49, 54-55, 1109-10.

who had himself attacked slavery in print a few years before Paine's arrival in America. Rush, a friend of John Adams and other members of Congress and of the renowned artisan scientist David Rittenhouse, was already advocating in private the establishment of an independent American republic. Friendships like this and his position as editor of the *Pennsylvania Magazine* allowed Paine to elaborate and refine his ideas in the charged political atmosphere of Philadelphia. By the end of his first year in America he was familiar with the issues and arguments of the colonists' conflict with Britain and was ready to enlist his literary talent in the cause of independence and republicanism.

The political situation at the close of 1775 was confused and ironic. War between British troops and Americans had broken out in Massachusetts in April, and in May the Second Continental Congress gathered in Philadelphia, bringing to the city not only the Adams cousins but such illustrious Virginians as George Washington, Thomas Jefferson, Richard Henry Lee and Patrick Henry. Throughout the summer Pennsylvania, like the other provinces, actively enlisted troops, and military engagements against the British were fought in New England and the South. At the same time debate raged in Congress between advocates of vigorous opposition to the mother country and friends of reconciliation, led by Pennsylvania's Galloway and John Dickinson, no longer in the forefront of Whig ranks. In November, Congress learned that the British government had refused to receive the conciliatory Olive Branch Petition it had approved the previous July, and in December, the delegates authorized the importation of gunpowder and munitions and the construction of an American navy.

These developments undermined the possibility of reconciliation, and strengthened the hand of the Adamses, Rush and other advocates of separation from Britain. But there were also powerful forces militating against independence. To begin with, the seeming impossibility of defeating the most powerful military authority in the world strengthened the natural reluctance of men to embrace treason. And there were the tradition of obedience to British rule and the protection Americans enjoyed as past of the British Empire. Many of the wealthy merchants, planters and lawyers who dominated Congress, moreover, were alarmed at the upsurge of popular participation in politics which had accompanied the creation of extra-legal non-importation committees in 1774 and 1775. They feared that war and independence would unleash a movement for political change within the colonies themselves. Despite the fact that war was in progress and British authority was in fact suspended, most political leaders still vindicated their actions by invoking the "rights of Englishmen" rather than the goal of independence and the hope persisted that a peaceful accommodation could be reached. As Paine observed, the situation was "strangely astonishing, perfect independence contending for dependence."[3]

It was Paine's *Common Sense,* published in January 1776, which transformed the terms of political debate. Benjamin Rush suggested to Paine that he write a pamphlet broaching the subject of independence, although he specifically warned Paine to avoid both that word and republicanism—advice Paine chose to ignore. At first, no typographer would agree to set the pamphlet in print, but finally the "republican printer" Robert Bell (a notorious Scot who openly kept a mistress and was one of Philadelphia's most enterprising businessmen) agreed. While Rush gave the pamphlet its name and he, Franklin, Rittenhouse, Sam Adams and possibly one or two others read the manuscript and made a few minor changes, the arguments and the means of presenting them were Paine's. He was fully responsible for "the most brilliant pamphlet written during the American Revolution, and one of the most brilliant pamphlets ever written in the English language."[4]

"My motive and object in all my political works, beginning with *Common Sense,*" Paine recalled in 1806, "...have been to rescue man from tyranny and false systems and false principles of gov-

[3]Foner, *Complete Writings,* I, 43; Miller, *Origins,* 416-17, 422, 446, 459.

[4]Worthington C. Ford, ed., "Letters of William Duane," *Proceedings,* Massachusetts Historical Society, 2 ser., XX (1906-07), 279; L.H. Butterfield, ed., *Letters of Benjamin Rush* (2 vols.: Philadelphia, 1951), II, 1007; John A. Schutz and Douglass Adair, eds., *The Spur of Fame: Dialogues of John Adams and Benjamin Rush, 1805-1813* (San Marino, Cal., 1966), 151; *Pa. Evening Post,* February 22, 1776; Daniel J. Boorstin, *The Americans: The Colonial Experience* (New York, 1959), 309; Bernard Bailyn, "Common Sense," *American Heritage,* XXV (December, 1973), 36.

ernment, and enable him to be free." Paine began *Common Sense*
not with a discussion of America's relations with Britain, but with
an analysis of the principles of government and an attack on
hereditary rule and the validity of monarchy itself. Paine always
considered the republican argument of *Common Sense* more important than the pamphlet's call for independence. "The mere
independence of America," he later wrote, "were it to have been
followed by a system of government modelled after the corrupt
system of English Government, would not have interested me
with the unabated ardor it did. It was to bring forward and establish the representative system of government, as the work
itself will show, that was the leading principle with me in writing."

There had been a few attacks on hereditary authority and calls
for republican government in the colonial press before Paine
wrote. But, by and large, republicanism had existed as an unarti-
culated strain of political radicalism and as a component of the
evangelical religious mind. The Country party ideologists whose
outlook dominated the writings of previous colonial pamphleteers had not challenged the view that the British constitution,
with its balance between monarch, Lords and Commons, was the
most perfect system of government in the world, even while they
warned that "corruption" was undermining the stability of this
finely tuned structure. In *Common Sense,* Paine literally transformed the political language. "Republic" had previously been
used as a term of abuse in political writing; Paine made it a living
political issue and a utopian ideal of government.[5]

Paine's savage attack on "the so much boasted Constitution of
England" contains the most striking passages in *Common Sense.*
He not only raised the by now traditional cry that corruption was
destroying English liberty, but he denounced the whole notion of
the historical legitimacy of the monarchy itself. His description of
the accession of William the Conqueror seven centuries earlier

[5]Foner, *Complete Writings,* II, 1480; Gordon S. Wood, *The Creation of the
American Republic, 1776-1787* (Chapel Hill, 1969); 199-200, 223; W. Paul Adams,
"Republicanism in Political Rhetoric Before 1776," *Political Science Quarterly,*
LXXXV (September, 1970), 398-404; Pauline Maier, *From Resistance to Revolu-
tion* (New York, 1972), 288-95; Pauline Maier, "The Beginnings of American
Republicanism," in *The Development of a Revolutionary Mentality* (Washing-
ton, 1972), 99-104.

would become one of his most frequently quoted passages: "A French bastard landing with an armed banditti and establishing himself king of England against the consent of the natives, is in plain terms a very paltry rascally original. ... The plain truth is that the antiquity of the English monarchy will not bear looking into." Paine minced no words in his assaults on the principle of hereditary rule: "Of more worth is one honest man to society, and in the sight of God, than all the crowned ruffians that ever lived." And: "One of the strongest natural proofs of the folly of hereditary right in kings is that nature disproves it, otherwise she would not so frequently turn it into ridicule, by giving mankind *an ass for a lion.*" Far from being the most perfect system of government in the world, the king was "the royal brute of England" and the English constitution simply "the base remains of two ancient tyrannies, compounded with some new Republican materials...the remains of monarchial tyranny in the person of the king... the remains of aristocratical tyranny in the persons of the peers."[6]

Paine was the first writer in America to denounce the English constitution so completely, and with it the idea that balanced government was essential to liberty. To be sure, he could use the familiar language of the Commonwealthmen in denouncing the British government: "in its present state...the corrupt influence of the Crown, by having all the places in its disposal, hath...effectively swallowed up the power, and eaten up the virtue of the House of Commons." But he differed from contemporary radicals, both in England and America, in idealizing neither the uncorrupted, balanced constitution, nor some mythical Anglo-Saxon past (although his attack on William the Conqueror by implication invoked the popular tradition of the "Norman Yoke"). Instead, Paine simply urged the establishment of republican government in America, while only hinting at its structure. Paine was always more interested in principles than forms of government, but he did call for the creation of a continental legislature and new unicameral state assemblies based on a broad suffrage, popular representation through frequent elections, and a written

[6]Foner, *Complete Writings,* I, 4-16, 29.

constitution guaranteeing the rights of persons and property and establishing freedom of religion.[7]

Common Sense then turned to a discussion of independence, an issue that had been mentioned sporadically in the press in 1775, but one which most colonists still refused to confront. One by one, Paine considered and then demolished the arguments for reconciliation. Was it ungrateful to rebel since Britain was "the parent country"? "The more shame upon her conduct," answered Paine. "Even brutes do not devour their young, nor savages make war upon their own families." Moreover, Paine insisted, it was wrong to consider England "the parent country of America" since "this new world hath been the asylum for the persecuted lovers of civil and religious liberty from *every part of Europe.*" Was America weak in comparison to Britain? Quite the reverse, Paine declared. "There is something absurd in supposing a continent to be perpetually governed by an island." Would independence involve America in wars with European powers while depriving it of British protection? "France and Spain," Paine replied, "never were, nor perhaps ever will be, our enemies as *Americans,* but as our being the subjects of Great Britain." America should "steer clear of European connections, which she can never do" while imprisoned in the British empire. It was monarchial government which caused the wars which perennially afflicted Europe, while "the republics of Europe are all ... in peace."[8]

Paine also addressed himself to conservatives who, he said, "dreaded an independence, fearing that it would produce civil wars." Independence, he replied, was inevitable. Since the outbreak of war, all plans for reconciliation "are like the almanacks of the last years; which though proper then, are superceded and useless now." The only question was how independence would come—"by the legal voice of the people in Congress; by a military

[7]Bernard Bailyn, *The Ideological Origins of the American Revolution* (Cambridge, 1967), 285; E. P. Thompson, *The Making of the English Working Class* (London, 1963), 86-88; Foner, *Complete Writings,* I, 6, 28; Hawke, *Paine,* 43-44; Christopher Hill, "The Norman Yoke," in Hill, *Puritanism and Revolution* (London, 1958), 50-122.

[8]J. M. Bumsted, "'Things in the Womb of Time': Ideas of American Independence, 1633 to 1763," *William and Mary Quarterly,* 3 ser., XXXI (October, 1974), 533-64; Maier, *Resistance to Revolution,* 266-68; Foner, *Complete Writings,* 16-21, 25-26, 32, 41, 44, 400.

power; or by a mob." In effect, Paine was warning conservatives that the very "popular disquietudes" they feared would produce internal upheaval might, if unfulfilled, be harnessed by demagogues in an uprising which would "finally sweep away the liberties of the continent like a deluge. ... Ye that oppose independence now, ye know not what ye do: ye are opening a door to eternal tyranny."[9]

"I challenge the warmest advocate for conciliation," Paine declared, "to show a single advantage that this continent can reap by being connected with Great Britain." Not only was America a plaything of British politicians and constantly involved in European disputes, but British mercantilist regulations were inimical to the economic growth of the colonies and responsible for "many material injuries." "No nation in a state of foreign dependence" and "limited in its commerce" could ever achieve "material eminence" or political greatness. Paine outlined a vision of an independent American empire, pursuing a policy of friendship and free trade with all nations, promoted by a strong continental government, complete with a national debt ("a national debt is a national bond") and a powerful navy.[10]

Toward the close of *Common Sense,* Paine moved beyond these material considerations to outline in lyrical rhetoric a breathtaking vision of the meaning of American independence. "We have it in our power to begin the world over again...the birthday of a new world is at hand." Paine transformed the struggle over the rights of Englishmen into a contest with meaning for all mankind:[11]

> O! ye that love mankind! Ye that dare oppose not only tyranny but the tyrant, stand forth! Every spot of the old world is overrun with oppression. Freedom hath been hunted round the globe. Asia and Africa have long expelled her. Europe regards her as a stranger, and England hath given her warning to depart. O! receive the fugitive, and prepare in time an asylum for mankind.

The immediate success and impact of *Common Sense* was nothing short of astonishing. At a time when the most widely circu-

[9]Foner, *Complete Writings,* I, 17-18, 24, 27-30, 45.

[10]Foner, *Complete Writings,* I, 18, 20, 32-34, 41. Cf. William Appleman Williams, *The Contours of American History* (London ed., 1961), 116-19.

[11]Foner, *Complete Writings,* I, 31, 45. Cf. Wood, *Creation,* 43-48, 91-118.

lated colonial newspapers were fortunate if they averaged two thousand sales per week, when the average pamphlet was printed in one or two editions of perhaps a few thousand copies, *Common Sense* went through twenty-five editions and reached literally hundreds of thousands of readers in the single year 1776. It also reached non-readers; one report from Philadelphia in February said the pamphlet "is read to all ranks." Paine later claimed *Common Sense* had sold at least 150,000 copies, and most historians have accepted this figure as roughly accurate. As Paine exulted, it was "the greatest sale that any performance ever had since the use of letters."[12]

From up and down the thirteen colonies in the spring of 1776 came reports that the pamphlet was read by "all sorts of people" and that it had made "innumerable converts" to independence. A Connecticut man announced, "You have declared the sentiments of millions. Your production may justly be compared to a land-flood that sweeps all before it. We were blind, but on reading these enlightening words the scales have fallen from our eyes." And from Philadelphia itself a writer in February 1776 commented on "the progress of the idea of Colonial independence in three weeks or a month," adding, "surely thousands and tens of thousands of common farmers and tradesmen must be better reasoners than some of our untrammelled *juris consultores,* who to this hour feel a reluctance to part with the abominable chain."[13]

John Adams always resented the fact that *Common Sense* was credited with having contributed so much to the movement for independence. Its discussion of that subject, he insisted, was simply "a tolerable summary of the arguments which I had been repeating again and again in Congress for nine months."[14] To some extent, Adams was right, but he failed to understand the genius of Paine's pamphlet. *Common Sense* did express ideas which had long circulated in the colonies—the separateness of America from Europe, the corruption of the Old World and in-

[12]Thomas R. Adams, *American Independence: The Growth of an Idea* (Providence, 1965), xi-xii; Foner, *Complete Writings,* II, 1162-63; Hawke, *Paine,* 47.

[13]*Pa. Evening Post,* February 13, March 26, 1776; Winthrop D. Jordan, "Familial Politics: Thomas Paine and the Killing of the King," *Journal of American History,* LX (September, 1973), 295; *Pa. Packet,* February 12, 1776.

[14]L. H. Butterfield, ed., *Diary and Autobiography of John Adams* (4 vols.: Cambridge, 1961), III, 333.

nocence of the New, the absurdity of hereditary privilege and the possibility of a future American empire. None of these ideas was original with Paine. What was brilliantly innovative was the way Paine combined them into a single comprehensive argument and related them to the common experiences of Americans.

Paine's reference to the colonists' diverse European origins and denial of England as the sole "parent country" was self-evident in a province like Pennsylvania, with its thoroughly heterogeneous population. His discussion of the benefits of isolation from the power struggles of the Old World was all but obvious to Americans who could remember that between 1689 and 1763 the colonies had been involved in four military conflicts between Britain and her European foes. His description of the virtues of republican government confirmed the experiences of colonists, especially in New England, who had long known a kind of republicanism in town meetings and annual elections, and of others who in 1774 and 1775 had witnessed the ability of popularly elected committees to exercise the functions of government. Paine's reference to the material benefits of free trade with Europe was especially persuasive in light of the high profits merchants and farmers had reaped by exporting grain to Portugal in the 1760s and 1770s. And his vision of a powerful American empire was attractive to Americans who had matured in an age of empires and felt an abiding interest in westward expansion. The most far-sighted colonists, like Benjamin Franklin, had long envisioned the New World as the site of a continental state exceeding in population and power any of the nations of Europe. (It is worth noting that Paine, Franklin and others used the word "empire" in its eighteenth-century sense of expanding territorial and commercial sovereignty, with none of the negative emotive implications of more modern usage. Paine, for example, helped to popularize the idea of a benevolent American empire while in 1778 condemning British rule in India as "not so properly a conquest as an extermination of mankind."[15])

[15]On the concept of an American empire, see William Appleman Williams, "The Age of Mercantilism: An Interpretation of the American Political Economy, 1763 to 1828," *William and Mary Quarterly,* 3 ser. (October, 1958), 419-21; R W. Van Alstyne, *The Rising American Empire* (New York, 1960), 1-6. Paine's comment is in Foner, *Complete Writings,* I, 119; he referred again to "the probability of empire" in 1779 (II, 202).

Equally striking was the way Paine enlisted the Bible-based Protestantism of the majority of colonists in the cause of republicanism and independence. Near the beginning of *Common Sense* are several paragraphs with lengthy Biblical quotations designed to show that monarchy was incompatible with true Christianity and the word of God. "The will of the Almighty," he concluded, "...expressly disapproves of government by kings." Monarchy was "the most prosperous invention the devil ever set on foot for the promotion of idolatry.... [It is] in every instance...the popery of government." It may seem ironic that Paine, who twenty years hence condemned the authority of the Bible in *The Age of Reason,* would use such arguments. When John Adams told Paine he thought the Biblical reasoning in *Common Sense* was ridiculous, Paine laughed, "expressed a contempt of the Old Testament and indeed the Bible at large" and announced his intention of one day publishing a work on religion.[16]

However tedious the Biblical arguments of *Common Sense* may seem to the modern reader, however disingenuous Paine may have been in these passages, he understood only too well the necessity of stripping monarchy of its Biblical authority and appealing to the anti-Popery sentiments which suffused the culture of eighteenth-century American and English Protestants, who viewed the Catholic Church as the essence of despotic hierarchy and the denial of individual liberty and self-direction. He utilized Biblical imagery and language throughout the pamphlet, as in his appeal to conservatives, "ye know not what ye do," and his description of the King of England as a "Pharoah." And he invoked, in a secularized form, the millennial hope for the coming of a new world, the vision of a perfect society, which had been "predominant among English-speaking Protestants since the later seventeenth century." Paine transformed the language of an impending millennium into the secular vision of a utopia in the New World. To the millennial view of the American past as a stage in the process whereby God's kingdom would be established on this earth, Paine added the future destiny of America as a society defined by its commitment to liberty and its isolation from the Old World. Paine's image of a New World "could only be

[16]Foner, *Complete Writings,* I, 10-12; Butterfield, ed., *Adams Diary,* III, 333.

created by a man who knew Europe well enough to hate its society and who longed desperately enough for salvation to envision in a flash of illumination the destiny of the New World as liberation from the Old."[17]

John Adams, as we have seen, considered Paine's arguments in *Common Sense* to have been singularly unoriginal. Nothing in the pamphlet was new, he believed, except "the phrases, suitable for an emigrant from New Gate, or one who had chiefly associated with such company, such as 'the royal brute of England,' 'the blood upon his soul,' and not a few others of equal delicacy." Adams was certainly correct in believing that that uniqueness of Paine's pamphlet lay not simply in broaching the hitherto forbidden subjects of independence and republicanism, but in doing so in a new literary tone and style. But he once again failed to recognize the significance of Paine's achievement. If the era of the Revolution witnessed "the massive politicization of American society," *Common Sense,* written in a style designed to reach a mass audience, was central to the explosion of political argument and involvement beyond the confines of a narrow elite to "all ranks" of Americans.[18]

The first thing which contemporaries noticed about *Common Sense* was its tone of outrage. Consider Paine's description of his reaction to the outbreak of hostilities at Lexington and Concord:

> No man was a warmer wisher for a reconciliation than myself, before the fatal nineteenth of April, 1775, but the moment the event of that day was made known, I rejected the hardened, sullen-tempered Pharoah of England for ever; and disdain the wretch, that with the pretended title of Father of his People can unfeelingly hear of their slaughter, and composedly sleep with their blood upon his soul.

What contemporaries described as Paine's "daring impudence" and "uncommon frenzy" was far removed from the legalistic,

[17]Ernest Lee Tuveson, *Redeemer Nation: The Idea of America's Millennial Role* (Chicago, 1968), 11-12, 20-24, 34-37; Yehoshura Arieli, *Individualism and Nationalism in American Ideology* (Cambridge, 1964), 71-73, 269-70.

[18]John R. Howe, *From the Revolution Through the Age of Jackson* (Englewood Cliffs, 1973), 28-31; Margaret Willard, ed., *Letters on the American Revolution 1774-1776* (Boston and New York, 1925), 274.

logical arguments, the "decorous and reasonable" language, of previous American political pamphlets.[19]

But there was more to Paine's appeal than the enraged assaults on hereditary monarchy that so offended Adams and the "indecent expressions" to which Henry Laurens of South Carolina objected. Paine was the conscious pioneer of a new style of political writing, a rhetoric aimed at extending political discussion beyond the narrow bounds of the eighteenth-century's "political nation." "As it is my design to make those that can scarcely read understand," he once wrote, "I shall therefore avoid every literary ornament and put it in language as plain as the alphabet." He assumed knowledge of no authority but the Bible, provided immediate translations for the few Latin phrases he employed and avoided florid language designed to impress more cultivated readers.

Paine was capable, to be sure, of creating brilliant metaphors, such as his famous reply in *The Rights of Man* to Edmund Burke's sympathy for the fate of Marie Antoinette: "He pities the plumage, but forgets the dying bird." He could employ humor as a weapon, as when he observed in *Common Sense* that American grain would "always have a market while eating is the custom of Europe." But the hallmarks of his writing were clarity, directness and forcefulness. His vocabulary and grammar were straightforward, and he carried his readers along with great care from one argument to the next. A good example of how he constructed his argument is the beginning of the discussion of monarchy in *Common Sense*. Paine had alluded to the social distinction between rich and poor, and then went on:[20]

> But there is another and greater distinction for which no truly natural or religious reason can be assigned, and that is the distinction of men into Kings and Subjects. Male and Female are the

---

[19] Foner, *Complete Writings*, I, 25; Bailyn, "Common Sense," 36-39; Bailyn, *Ideological Origins*, 12-19; Charles Inglis, *The True Interest of America* (Philadephia, 1776), 34.

[20] Elisha P. Douglass, *Rebels and Democrats* (Chapel Hill, 1955), 21; Foner, *Complete Writings,* II, 111; I, 260, 9, 18. Cf. Paine's footnote after using the word "soliloquy" in an April 1776 newspaper article: "As this piece may possibly fall into the hands of some who are not acquainted with the word soliloquy, for their information the sense of it is given, viz. 'talking to one's self.'" Foner, II, 74.

distinctions of nature, good and bad the distinctions of heaven; but how a race of men came into the world so exalted above the rest, and distinguished like some new species, is worth inquiring into, and whether they are the means of happiness or misery to the world.

Paine was not the first writer of the eighteenth century consciously to address himself to a wide readership. There are similarities between his literary style and the "plain English," the "clear and easy prose" of English novelists such as Defoe and Richardson and political essayists like Addison, Swift and Junius. Each of these writers developed modes of literary expression addressed to "the plain understanding of the people," elucidated the "plain truth," and drew on the everyday experiences of their readers. (Paine, in fact, originally planned to title his pamphlet *Plain Truth,* but was convinced by Benjamin Rush to call it *Common Sense.*) Nor was Paine the first pamphleteer in England or America to use outrageous and even insulting language. In several colonial electoral contests, including the Philadelphia campaign of 1764, political opponents hurled invective at one another. Paine himself was acquainted with the biting personal satire of Junius in England. But unlike Junius, whose writing was at its best when it attacked prominent individuals, Paine announced at the outset of *Common Sense* his intention of avoiding "everything which is personal" and all "compliments as well as censure to individuals."[21] Paine's concern was not with personalities, but with the principles of government. And his rage was tempered by a conscious effort to engage the reason as well as the passions of his readers. His savage attacks on kingship and his careful exposition of the essential principles of republicanism were two sides of the same coin: both were meant to undermine the entire system of deferential politics.

Paine's message, stated explicitly and conveyed by his tone and rhythm as well as his appeals to common experience, was that anyone could grasp the nature of politics and government. He flaunted his contempt for precedent and authority. "In this part

[21] Ian Watt, *The Rise of the Novel* (London, 1957), 29-30, 54-59, 101-04, 194-96; James T. Boulton, *The Language of Politics in the Age of Wilkes and Burke* (London, 1963), 19-23, 52, 252; James T. Boulton, ed., *Daniel Defoe* (New York, 1965), 2-9, 15; Hawke, *Paine,* 44; Gary B. Nash, "The Transformation of Urban Politics, 1700-1765," *Journal of American History,* LX (December, 1973), 619-20.

of the debate," Paine wrote in the spring of 1776 of a newspaper antagonist, "Cato shelters himself chiefly in quotations from other authors, without reasoning much on the matter himself; in answer to which, I present him with a string of maxims and recollections, drawn from the nature of things, without borrowing from any one." Rather than invoking authorities and legal precedents, Paine offered "nothing more than simple facts, plain arguments, and common sense." Politics, Paine insisted, could and must be reduced to easily comprehensible first principles: "Notwithstanding the mystery with which the science of government has been enveloped, for the purpose of enslaving, plundering and imposing upon mankind, it is of all things the least mysterious and the most easy to be understood." And the first axiom of Paine's politics was simply the possibility of change. Men could, by the exercise of reason, throw off the dead weight of tradition and see "government begin, as if we lived in the beginning of time."[22]

To his critics, Paine was as guilty of debasing the language as of attacking the government. Gouverneur Morris scoffed at him as "a mere adventurer...without fortune, without family or connexions, ignorant even of grammar" (a remark seemingly more appropriate to a patronage society like Britain than to colonial America). Even Franklin, sending a publication of Paine's to a friend in Paris, felt obliged to remark, "This rude way of writing in America will seem strong on your side." But Paine was indeed a conscious artist, who agonized over his choice of words and wrote and rewrote with great care. He was aware that he was creating a style of writing, "hitherto unknown on this side of the Atlantic," as Virginia's Edmund Randolph put it. Most writers of the eighteenth century believed that to write for a mass audience meant to sacrifice refinement for coarseness and triviality, to reject a "high" or "literary" style in favor of a "low" or "vulgar" one. The American pamphleteers before Paine, with rare exceptions, came from the upper social strata of lawyers, merchants, planters and ministers. Only Paine had sprung from that same mass audience which devoured his works on both sides of the Atlantic. His literary style, his rejection of deference and his political

[22]Foner, *Complete Writings*, II, 78; I, 17, 376, 571.

republicanism were all interdependent: for Paine, the medium was of one piece with the message.[23]

In February 1776, the Massachusetts Whig Joseph Hawley read *Common Sense* and remarked: "Every sentiment has sunk into my well prepared heart." The hearts of Hawley and thousands of other Americans had been readied for Paine's arguments by the extended conflict over Britain's right to tax the colonies, the outbreak of war and the pervasive influence of the Country party vision of a corrupt British government and society. The intensification of fighting in the winter of 1775-76—the American invasion of Canada, the burning of Falmouth, Maine by the British, the bombardment of Norfolk coupled with Lord Dunmore's attempt to arm Virginia slaves to fight against the colonists and the arrival of news of the British decision to send German mercenaries to serve beside her own soldiers—all gave added weight to Paine's call for independence. As George Washington observed, "A few more of such flaming arguments as were exhibited at Falmouth and Norfolk, added to the sound doctrine and unanswerable reasoning contained in the pamphlet *Common Sense,* will not leave members [of Congress] at a loss to decide upon the propriety of separation."

Common Sense did not, of course, "cause" either the movement or the decision for independence. Six months would elapse after its publication until Congress approved the Declaration of Independence. But the pamphlet's astonishing impact stemmed from the fact that it appeared at precisely the moment when Americans were ready to accept Paine's destruction of arguments favoring conciliation and his appeal to latent republicanism, to the material

[23]Foner, *Complete Writings,* I, xviii; Franklin quoted in Benjamin Vaughan to Lord Shelburne, December 26, 1782 (copy), Gimbel Collection, American Philosophical Society; "Edmund Randolph's Essay," *Virginia Magazine of History and Biography,* XLIII (1935), 306; Bailyn, *Ideological Origins,* 13-17. My analysis of Paine's literary style has been influenced by the excellent discussions in Thompson, *Making of the English Working Class,* 90-92; Harry Hayden Clark, "Thomas Paine's Theories of Rhetoric," *Transactions,* Wisconsin Academy of Sciences, Arts and Letters, XXVIII (1933), 307-09; J. H. Plumb, "The Public, Literature and the Arts in the Eighteenth Century," in Paul Fritz and David Williams, eds., *The Triumph of Culture: Eighteenth Century Perspectives* (Toronto, 1972), 27-48; and especially, Boulton, *Language of Politics.*

interests of the colonists and to the widespread idealistic hopes for the future of the New World. Paine articulated the deepest meaning of the struggle with Britain for an audience still preoccupied with attaining the full rights of Englishmen, and drew new secular, republican conclusions from such deep traditions of popular thought as anti-Popery and the "Norman Yoke." By doing all this in a new style of writing and a new political language, Paine "broke the ice that was slowly congealing the revolutionary movement."[24] The success of *Common Sense* reflected the perfect conjunction of a man and his time, a writer and his audience, and it announced the emergence of Paine as the outstanding political pamphleteer of the Age of Revolution.

[24]James T. Austin, *The Life of Elbridge Gerry* (Boston, 1859), 163; Hawke, *Paine,* 47; Miller, *Origins,* 467.

Thomas Jefferson and the Equality of Man[1]

by Garry Wills

There is no minimizing Jefferson's views on Negro limits. He catalogued what he saw as multiple inferiorities in the first and only book he ever published *(Notes,* 138-43).[2] The black's weak points are listed with a ruthless scrutiny meant to impress the philosophes of France. Blacks lack intelligence, beauty, most skills except music. Perhaps the most damaging item within Jefferson's own scheme of things is the claim that they are weak in Hutcheson's "inner sense" of aesthetic delight at finer things. Jefferson approaches the whole Negro phenomenon with the air of a Buffon studying some rare insect, though his vocabulary comes closer to Dr. Johnson's:

> They secrete less by the kidnies, and more by the glands of the skin, which gives them a very strong and disagreeable odour. This greater degree of transpiration renders them more tolerant of heat, and less so of cold, than the whites. Perhaps too a difference of structure in the pulmonary apparatus, which a late ingenious experimentalist

[1][References included in the text have been reproduced exactly as they appear in *Inventing America.* The footnotes at the bottom of the page have been added by the editor, and are based on the information provided in the "Key to Brief Citations," pages 372-73 of *Inventing America.* — Ed.]

[2][Reference is to Thomas Jefferson, *Notes on the State of Virginia,* ed. William Peden (New York, 1972). Page numbers are given in the text. — Ed.]

has discovered to be the principal regulator of animal heat, may have disabled them from extricating, in the act of inspiration, so much of that fluid from the outer air, or obliged them in expiration to part with more of it (139).

Whether the black of the negro resides in the reticular membrane between the skin and scarf skin, or in the scarf skin itself; whether it proceeds from the colour of the blood, the colour of the bile, or from that of some other secretion, the difference is fixed in nature. ...(138).

Nor did Jefferson think these differences were caused by education or conditioning—i.e., by slavery itself—since white slaves under the Romans did not exhibit the same disabilities. When Jefferson denies that their condition can explain blacks' limits, the modern student is apt to remark that Jefferson's own conditioning is at work here, making him inconsistent in theory because he was guilty in practice. The slaveowner speaks, not the scientist.

But David Hume neither preached nor practiced slavery, and his attempts at a scientific conclusion on this matter are similar to Jefferson's:

I am apt to suspect the Negroes to be naturally inferior to the whites. There scarcely ever was a civilized nation of that complexion, nor even any individual eminent either in action or speculation. No ingenious manufactures among them, no arts, no sciences. On the other hand, the most rude and barbarous of the whites, such as the ancient Germans, the present Tartars, have still something eminent about them, in their valor, form of government, or some other particular. Such a uniform and constant difference could not happen, in so many countries and ages, if nature had not made an original distinction between these breeds of men. Not to mention our colonies, there are Negro slaves dispersed all over Europe, of whom none ever discovered any symptoms of ingenuity; though low people, without education, will start up amongst us, and distinguish themselves in every profession. In Jamaica, indeed, they talk of one Negro as a man of arts and learning; but it is likely he is admired for slender accomplishments, like a parrot who speaks a few words plainly ("Of National Characters," 1748).

A modern reader may find Jefferson's views most shocking when he claims that black men admit white superiority through "their own preference of them [white women], as uniform as is the preference of the oran-ootan for the black women over those of his own species" (138). Here is confusion of species indeed, with orangutans lusting after black women as black men lust after white women. The crazed sexuality that haunts so much of black-white relations in our history seems to derange with a leer Jefferson's pose of scientific observation. Even our best student of racial attitudes in American history, Winthrop Jordan, refers to this "gratuitous intrusion of the man-like ape," and says that Jefferson wrote this passage with a "geyser of libidinal energy" *(White Over Black,* 458-59).

But Jordan himself documents the fascination orangutans exercised over philosophes. (And see Robert Workler, *Studies on Voltaire,* vol. 155.) The tailless chimpanzee posed the most immediate challenge to the taxonomists' separation of animal species. The eighteenth century lived in a seizure of cataloguing impulses (to which Jefferson was especially susceptible), and the orangutan seemed hard to place in the known systems. The great systemizer of the time, the Comte de Buffon, was puzzled for a while by this effort to place the orangutan (Jordan, 230), and one of the things that puzzled him most was the credible report of mating between women and orangutans. (The intercourse was always between male chimp and female human—not only because males were presumed to have the fiercer sexual drive, but because women were less able to beat off an assailant by sheer strength.) These widespread tales were not more astonishing than many travelers' reports that gained acceptance during and after the age of exploration.

Evidence of cross-breeding had a more than prurient interest for an age experimenting with hybridization, after the example of Linnaeus. The possibility of fertility in the product of an ape-woman mating not only threatened the division of species; it led to speculation that some known creatures (the orangutan and the Hottentot were the favorite candidates) were themselves the product of such unions. Diderot tells the story of Cardinal Polignac addressing the famous orangutan (observed by Jefferson) in the Paris Zoo: "But speak and I baptize you" *(Rêve de d'Alembert,* Pléiade, 941). That passage in Diderot is interesting because it shows that the more daring philosophes were willing to challenge the Church's ban on "bestiality" (sex with animals): Diderot defends what has come to be called polymorphous sexuality (935-42) as the logical consequence of his view that sensation should "accord" one to all the vibrating fibers of the universe.

By telling the story of Cardinal Polignac, Diderot recalls debates on the advisability of baptizing the various kinds of "natives" found by explorers in distant places—Hottentots, pygmies, Negroes, Indians, etc. The question was not only, Are these men, but Are they descendants of Adam? Perhaps there were other races of men outside the Fall of Adam, and needing no redemption. God could have made several Edens; and even if these Edens, too, gave evidence of a fall, they were not in the economy of redemption by Christ if they had not fallen in the first Adam.

At the point where Hottentot seemed to dwindle into orangutan, where (if anywhere) could a distinction be drawn? A typical answer is that of Sir Richard Blackmore in *The Lay Monastery* (1714), cited by Arthur Lovejoy as an example of the Enlightenment's approach to the orangutan:

> The ape, or the monkey that bears the greatest similitude to man, is the next order of animals below him. Nor is the disagreement between the basest individuals of our species and the ape or monkey so great but that, were the latter endowed with the faculty of speech ["But speak, and I baptize you"], they might perhaps as justly claim the rank and dignity of the human race as the savage Hottentot or stupid native of Nova Zembla. ... The most perfect of this order of beings, the orang-outang as he is called by the natives of Angola—that is, the Wild Man, or Man of the Woods—has the honor of bearing the greatest resemblance to human nature. Though all that species have some agreement with us in our features, many instances being found of men with monkey faces, yet this has the greatest likeness, not only in his countenance, but in the structure of his body, his ability to walk upright, as well as on all fours, his organs of speech, his ready apprehension, and his gentle and tender passions, which are not found in any of the ape kind, and in various other respects *(The Great Chain of Being,* 234-35).

The similarities between animals—including the human animal—were topics of *"philosophie"* because the common basis of sensation had taken on new importance in the wake of Locke. For men like Helvétius, to whom *"juger est sentir" (De l'esprit,* 1, i), the animal basis of human action—and even human thought— had brought men very close to beasts in the chain of being. This was a line of research that fascinated Jefferson all his life and made him follow the theories of Pierre-Jean-Georges Cabanis and the research of Pierre Flourens with enthusiastic approval (Cappon, 562, 564, 605-6).[3] Hume devoted a chapter of his *Enquiry Concerning Human Understanding* to "The Reason of Animals," concluding: "Though the instinct be different, yet still it is an instinct which teaches a man to avoid the fire, as much as that which teaches a bird, with such exactness, the art of incubation and the whole economy and order of its nursery."

Diderot went farther in approximating man to a bird:

> First [in the egg] there is a wavering speck, a lengthening and darkening thread, fleshing itself out, beak, wing-tips, eyes, claws becoming visible. A yellowish substance arranges itself into intestines. It is animate. The animal moves, thrashes, peeps—I can hear it through the shell! It becomes furry; it looks about. The heaviness of its wavering head throws the beak repeatedly against the inner prison-wall—see it broken through! It emerges, walks, flies, is sensitive to irritants, skits off, comes near; it moans, suffers, loves, yearns, plays. It has all your affections. All you can do, it does *(Rêve de d'Alembert,* Pléiade, 881).

One reason Diderot admired Greuze so much was their shared "sentimentality," which was actually sensationalism in the post-Locke sense. Greuze fits out the "natural" family with dogs and cats and birds that guard and play with the children, teaching adults a proper responsiveness to instinct. Greuze not only paints propaganda for the encyclopedist cause of breast-feeding; he has dogs menace the nurse who tries to take off the child, and he includes dogs nursing their young in pictures of family affection. In his "Portrait of Comtesse Molline," one pup of the newborn litter even nuzzles the breast of the girl holding it. The continuity of the animal spectrum is repeatedly emphasized. If the mediaeval world had its symbolic "bestiaries," so did the Enlightenment— and both were constructed for moral instruction.

Jefferson's use of the orangutan in his extensive effort to "place"

[3][See Lester J. Cappon, ed., *The Adams-Jefferson Letters* (Chapel Hill, 1959). —Ed.]

the Negro is not, therefore "gratuitous." We may think it unfortunate; but it was also inevitable. Not to note this well-known "fact" would have been ·considered remiss in a discussion of Negro faculties and their closest analogues. That is why an ardent opponent of slavery like Dr. Rush felt obliged, even while defending the equality of black and white human beings, to admit that black women had been raped by orangutans *(American Philosophical Society Transactions,* 4:291). Dr. Charles White, a physician who had seen the results of vegetable cross-breeding, remained skeptical that the orangutan matings with women (which he assumed had occurred) could produce offspring *(An Account of the Regular Gradation of Man,* 1799, 11-12). Jordan lists (236-37) others who took the union of women with orangutans as an adequately reported fact and then discussed the scientific consequences of this phenomenon. The boldness of investigation that men celebrate in the Enlightenment, the openness to all new things, led to the kind of conjecture Jordan calls "gratuitous" in Jefferson. It should be remembered that Jefferson was addressing the French philosophes in his book. Though written in answer to a request by Barbé-Marbois, it was aimed especially at Buffon, to challenge his theories about America's climate and wild life. When Jefferson talked of matings with orangutans, he was addressing a man who had already admitted that "fact" into his great *Histoire Naturelle.*

Enlightenment schemes of education turned to animal example for the discovery of nature's method in training the young. Thomas Reid urged this *(Enquiry,* 249-50) as a corollary of his teaching that doctors should imitate nature's healing process. Perhaps the most thorough discussion of this commonplace among Scottish philosophes was written by William Small's teacher, Dr. John Gregory. His *Comparative View of the State and Faculties of Man with Those of the Animal World,* published in 1765 in two volumes, provided a remarkably "permissive" guide to child-rearing; it was the Dr. Spock handbook of its day. Parents were urged not to force knowledge on children too early or by punishment (1:98 ff.) Sociability should be strengthened by loving care; the mother should fondle and breast-feed her child, preferably for a year: "When a mother does not nurse her own infant, she does open violence to nature" (1:44). It was vital to Gregory's thesis that men should resemble other animals in his faculties and upbringing. As he put it: "One species often runs into another so imperceptibly that it is difficult to say where the one begins and the other ends. This is particularly the case with the lowest of one species and the highest of that immediately below it" (1:11).

Still, there *is* a basis for the distinction between other animals and man; and Gregory proves he is a good member of the Scottish school when he tells us what that is: "Above all, they [men] are distinguished [from other animals] by the moral sense, and the happiness flowing from religion and from the various intercourses of social life" (1:16). The piety and sociability that end that list are simply different aspects of the moral sense. Man is distinguished from the beasts by his highest faculty—which, for the Scottish moral-sense philosopher, is not reason but benevolence, not the head but the heart.

This is, of course, Jefferson's position on the blacks:

> Whether further observation will or will not verify the conjecture that nature has been less bountiful to them in the endowments of the head, I believe that in those of the heart she will be found to have done them justice. That disposition to theft with which they have been branded, must be ascribed to their situation, and not to any depravity of the moral sense...we find among them numerous instances of the most rigid integrity, and as many as among their better instructed masters, of benevolence, gratitude, and unshaken fidelity *(Notes,* 142-43).

It is easy for a modern reader to think Jefferson has thrown an unimportant sop to the blacks with his praise for the "heart." After all, our culture takes reason and intellect to be the highest of man's faculties. Jefferson's Scottish mentors did not. To appreciate the real force of this passage, we must look at the technical meaning it had for Jefferson. This can be seen in three of its themes, put unmistakably in this brief statement of moral-sense doctrine.

First, the distinction of heart from head. This was a common enough distinction; but the reason it became so common in the eighteenth century was the weight several philosophical camps gave to it. And no camp took the matter more seriously than the Scottish moral-sense philosophers. For them, the heart was often another word for moral sense (as was benevolence, humanity, or sociability). In discussing the concept of natural rights, Hutcheson wrote: "The sense of everyone's heart, and the common natural principles, show that each one has these perfect rights; nor without maintaining them can there be any social life" (4:143 —cf. 2:315).[4] Adam Smith, making the normal Humean distinction between moral sense as the faculty that chooses *ends* and intellect as the one that chooses *means,* says that the highest human ideal is to unite these powers, benevolence with prudence: "It is the best head joined to the best heart. It is the most perfect wisdom combined with the most perfect virtue. It constitutes very nearly the character of the Academical or Peripatetic sage" *(Moral Sentiments,* 6, i). Perfection of the head is necessary to make the sage; but the faculty of the heart is the same in all men and makes them men.

Hume said that the head discerns fact and the heart discerns right, so that all *moral* blame must be directed at the heart: "The approbation or blame which then ensues cannot be the work of the judgment but of the heart; and it is not a speculative proposition or affirmation, but an active feeling or sentiment" *(Enquiry, Morals,* App. 1). Later, when discussing terms for separating "intellectual and moral endowments," he says: "The distinction between the heart and the head may also be adopted" (ibid., App. 4—cf. *Treatise,* 586, 603). We shall find that Jefferson's famous "head and heart" letter to Maria Cosway has been misread by eminent Jeffersonians because they failed to see how necessary, in the Scottish scheme, is the heart's superiority to the head, as the ground of right and dignity. The moral sense is not only man's *highest* faculty, but the one that is *equal* in all men.

A second proof that Jefferson is speaking in the strict terminology of Hutcheson comes from the list of virtues he recognizes in the Negro: "integrity...benevolence, gratitude, and unshaken fidelity" *(Notes,* 143). Hutcheson treated benevolence as the moral sense par excellence. It best illustrated the nonselfish aspect of that faculty. But benevolence can take other forms less obviously disinterested. These manifestations of the moral sense were less

---

[4][Reference is to the Georg Olms facsimile reprint of the *Collected Works* of Francis Hutcheson, 7 vols. (Hildesheim, 1971).—Ed.]

useful to the philosopher in establishing the nature of virtue. Gratitude, for instance, could be mistaken as a form of long-range selfishness, a *quid pro quo* for favors received. In the same way, honor could be taken for pride, or fidelity for caution. Only after he had established the mechanics of the moral sense as *benevolent* could he show that benevolence takes these other forms as well (1:197).

Gratitude was second in importance only to benevolence pure and simple. It figured largely in his original analysis, the 1725 *Inquiry* (1:50, 197-99), and it remained second in rank of all the moral virtues for him. Other theorists of the moral sense gave it similar rank (Smith, *Moral Sentiments,* 2, ii, 1; 3, iii, 6; Hume, *Treatise,* 603; *Enquiry, Morals,* 5, ii, App. 2). Even those Scottish thinkers who differed from Hutcheson on the exact meaning and rank of benevolence treated gratitude as one of the principal moral phenomena to be explained by moral science (Kames, *Principles,* 90; Reid, *Essays,* 1:149).

At first Hutcheson ranked honor third after benevolence and gratitude (1:200-3). It was the public virtue confirming sociability. But "fidelity" assumes that role in his later work, since faithfulness to contracts underlies all social transactions. "Fidelity" had the large sense of truth to commitments for Hutcheson—to marriage vows, friendship pledges, and national allegiance (4:177-79, 6:34-52). Hume understood it the same way (*Treatise,* 603, *Enquiry, Morals,* 6, i), as did Kames *(Principles,* 89). Jefferson's regard for it appears in the Declaration's protestation of "a faith yet unsullied."

Thus when Jefferson says that blacks are equal to whites in "benevolence, gratitude, and unshaken fidelity," he is listing the cardinal virtues of moral-sense theory, the central manifestations of man's highest faculty. What does he mean, however, by a fourth heading of his own, "the most rigid integrity"? Integrity was usually contrasted, in his day, with the kinds of political corruption Americans attributed to the British in their pamphlets on the Revolution. That does not seem appropriate when describing slaves. Once again, the explanation is to be found in the theorists of moral sense. Hutcheson used integrity as a synonym for his political virtue of fidelity: "By violating our faith we may quite defeat the desires of such as trusted to our integrity" (4:178). It belongs to that cluster of virtues variously described as "veracity, sincerity, fidelity," and contrasted with "falsehood, dissimulation, and deceit" (4:177). Hume, in the same way, spoke of "honesty, fidelity, truth" *(Enquiry, Morals,* 6, i). Thus Jefferson is recognizing in slaves, so often accused of compulsive lying, a basis for trust that lies behind all social compacts based on the moral sense.

The one criticism Jefferson deals with, raised against the assumption of equal moral sense in black slaves, is our third and in some ways most striking proof that he was talking about a literal equality of men. Jefferson refers to the slaves' well-known thieving ways. He was not exaggerating. It is actually a tribute to their skills that the slaves were successful in carrying out what Gerald Mullin describes as the masked rebellion of underground trade. The slaves at times controlled the chicken market so entirely that plantation owners had to buy their own chickens from their slaves. George Washington lamented that the slaves got two glasses of wine for every one served in the house; and he ordered all dogs shot at Mount Vernon because they served as sentinels for night raids on plantation stores (Mullin, *Flight and Rebellion,* 60-62). Plantation owners were understandably angered at these successes; but Jefferson will not let such acts stand as accusations of inequality. His answer not only acquits blacks of inferiority in this sense; it declares that blacks are not *bound* to any social arrangement, since they have been denied reciprocity:

> That disposition to theft with which they have been branded must be ascribed to their situation, and not to any depravity of the moral sense. The man, in whose favour no laws of property exist, probably feels himself less bound to respect those made in favour of others. When arguing for ourselves, we lay it down as a fundamental, that laws, to be just, must give a reciprocation of right [cf. Jefferson's denial that one can form a pact with oneself] : that, without this, they are mere arbitrary rules of conduct, founded in force, and not in conscience: and it is a problem which I give to the master to solve, whether the religious precepts against the violation of property were not framed for him as well as his slave? And whether the slave may not as justifiably take a little from one, who has taken all from him, as he may slay one who would slay him. ...Notwithstanding these considerations which must weaken their respect for the

laws of property, we find among them numerous instances of the most rigid integrity...*(Notes,* 142-43—cf. *Papers,* 14:492).[5]

Without the duty to live by fidelity to compact, blacks still manifest that virtue. This is very strong language for a Virginia plantation owner. In denying any duty to the social bond, he has asserted the right of rebellion. However timorous his own actions, he cannot justly be accused—as he so often is—of denying the same rights of revolution to blacks that he had proclaimed for whites.

Winthrop Jordan calls Jefferson inconsistent for using an environmental defense of blacks' thefts while denying that palliative to the blacks' intellectual gifts. But Jefferson's system did not commit him to equality of "mind and body" (as he put it to Chastellux, *Papers,* 8:186). He thought some men physically inferior (e.g., pygmies) and some superior (e.g., Indians). Like the majority of the philosophes he thought some men superior mentally— the Bacons and Lockes and Newtons—and some stunted, by original deprivation or evil circumstances (as whole cultures had been blighted by superstition and "priestcraft"). But these are minor differences by comparison with the faculty that gives man his unique dignity, that grounds his rights, that makes him self-governing. Equality of moral sense was not otherworldly, like equality of the soul in Christian thought. It was, Jefferson thought, a scientifically observable fact of our present life. Not even slavery and the evil nurture that promoted theft could hide the basic integrity and equality of blacks themselves.

When Jordan says that Jefferson taught later generations that "the Negro was to be judged on a thoroughly distinct matter—his intellectual capacity" (455), he fails to take with full seriousness just what Jefferson meant by the moral sense. Jordan, accusing Jefferson of emotional disturbance in his scientific inquiry, is carried away by emotion himself when he makes an accusation like this:

> Here at last, proclaimed in language at once passionate and clinical, was the Negro's true rank in nature's scale—exactly midway

---

[5][See Julian P. Boyd et al., *The Papers of Thomas Jefferson,* 19 vols. (Princeton, 1950-74).—Ed.]

> between ("as uniformly as") the white man and the most man-like
> ape. This connection with the ape was forged by Jefferson [*sic*] in
> his passage on the superior beauty of white women (490).

Most naturalists of Jefferson's day believed that orangutans had
raped black women; but most of them also believed in the equality
of men. They were not carried away by emotion at the report, as
Jordan allows himself to be. Jefferson was not original in his belief in the one or the other. But he did depart from some of those
naturalists in a programmatic insistence on the equality of the
moral sense, which was a liberating doctrine. Hutcheson, in his
introduction to morals, built his concept of political freedom and
equality entirely on the basis of *equal* moral faculty in all men:

> In this respect all men are originally equal, that these natural rights
> equally belong to all, at least as soon as they come to the mature use
> of reason; and they are equally confirmed to all by the law of
> nature. ... Nature makes none masters, none slaves (4:143-44).

Jefferson believed in a literal equality more far-reaching than
most educated people recognize today. For him, accidental differences of body or mind were dwarfed by an all-important equality in the governing faculty of man. There is no inconsistency in
his theory, whatever one may think of its validity. For him it was
valid, and everything he wrote about blacks in his extended
analysis for the *Notes* is derived from its principles.

"The Double-Tongued Deceiver": Sincerity and Duplicity in the Novels of Charles Brockden Brown

by Michael Davitt Bell

The four best-known novels of Charles Brockden Brown turn on a contest between two recurring figures: a virtuous but inexperienced protagonist (Clara Wieland, Constantia Dudley, Edgar Huntly, Arthur Mervyn) and an antagonist (Carwin, Ormond, Clithero Edny, Welbeck) whose attitudes and experience threaten the protagonist's conception of virtue and order. At the center of these novels is a dialectic between innocence and experience or, to use the terms Brown himself preferred, between "sincerity" and "duplicity." Brown's plots reveal the difficulty of living by honesty and idealism, a difficulty he had already noted in the early 1790's:

> I think it may safely be asserted that of all the virtues mankind is most universally deficient in sincerity. ....How many motives are there for concealing our real sentiment, for counterfeiting approbation and conviction? And how many occasions are there, on which, if its immediate and temporary effects only be considered, sincerity is criminal, and when a strict adherence to it would be, not only an infraction of politeness but a deviation from rectitude?[1]

[1]"Journal Letters to Henrietta G.," in David Lee Clark, *Charles Brockden Brown: Pioneer Voice of America* (Durham, N. C., 1952), p. 102. Clark dates these letters, which may in fact be a fragmentary draft of an epistolary novel, around 1790-93.

Here we see the curiously hypothetical reasoning from principle to complication that characterizes the novels. They present, in the figure of the antagonist, the logical and duplicitous extreme of that sincerity by which the protagonist attempts to live. It is in such terms that the central struggle of the novels must be understood.

The meaning of this struggle, however, may be approached in various ways. Brown's enthusiasm for such terms as "sincerity" — of great importance in the writings of Enlightenment political philosophers — has led some readers to emphasize the political side of his thought. To be sure, political ideas are important to Brown. In the late 1790's, during the very years in which his novels appeared, he was undergoing an intellectual transformation from radical idealism to pragmatic conservatism — from a belief in absolute sincerity to a recognition of the supremacy or inevitability of circumstance. And some of the antagonists in his novels, notably Carwin and Ormond, are linked with the excesses of the revolution in France. But such figures as Carwin and Ormond have little real political substance. Their schemes and ideals are vague and often quite preposterous. In his portrayal of them Brown substitutes melodramatic stereotype for serious political analysis.[2]

The real threat to the equanimity of Brown's protagonists seems to be psychological rather than political. As many readers have noted, Brown is centrally concerned with those forces that threaten eighteenth-century ideas of psychological order, ideas derived from Locke's *Essay Concerning Human Understanding.*

[2]It should be recognized that contemporary political discourse was at times as conventionally melodramatic as Brown's political villains. Thus Timothy Dwight could declare of the secret Order of the Illuminati, founded in Bavaria and popularly supposed to have caused the French Revolution and to be plotting similar disasters for America: "Adultery, assassination, poisoning, and other crimes of the like infernal nature, were taught as lawful, and even as virtuous actions." *(The Duty of Americans, at the Present Crisis* ...[New Haven, 1798] , p. 12.) On Brown's exploitation of popular alarm about the Illuminati see Lillie Deming Loshe, *The Early American Novel* (New York, 1907), pp. 41-43; and Clark, *Charles Brockden Brown,* pp. 188-92. On general American reaction to the Illuminati see Vernon Stauffer, *New England and the Bavarian Illuminati* (New York, 1918); and, for a briefer account, Howard Mumford Jones, *America and French Culture* (Chapel Hill, 1927), pp. 397-400.

For instance in *Wieland* (1798), Clara Wieland tells the story of her brother Theodore's growing insanity. At the behest of what he takes to be supernatural voices Theodore murders his wife and children and attempts to kill Clara. Clara attributes these voices to the ventriloquism of the mysterious intruder, Carwin. Her sense of psychological order is based on the Lockean model, in which all ideas and resulting motives derive from sense impressions, and in the course of the novel this model is undermined in two ways. Carwin's ventriloquism reveals the complexity and unreliability of the sensory apparatus, on which all else depends. And Wieland's insanity, which turns out to have arisen from his own mind and not from Carwin's deceptions, suggests a process of idea-formation quite outside Locke's theory of the mind. In psychological terms, then, *Wieland* portrays the contest between Lockean rationalism and the power of the irrational.[3]

Irrational psychology is important in *Wieland*. But tied to it is a more specific sense of what threatens Clara and her view of the world. What destroys the Wielands' idyllic American community is the force of imagination, of voices heard and visions seen in dreams. These dreams may represent the power of the repressed subconscious, but it should also be recalled that the Wieland family is related to "the modern poet of the same name." Their grandfather devoted his youth "to literature and music" and might be regarded, as Clara informs us, "as the founder of the German Theatre." (7)[4] These aspects of the Wieland family background suggest that among those irrational forces threatening Clara's sense of order is the force of literary art and literary imagination.

[3]See, for instance, Larzer Ziff, "A Reading of *Wieland*," *PMLA*, 77 (1962), 51-57. An earlier and fuller reading of *Wieland* along these lines is Chapter 5, "*Wieland:* Reason and Justice," in Warner Berthoff's "The Literary Career of Charles Brockden Brown," Diss. Harvard 1954. The fullest study of the breakdown of Lockean assumptions in all of Brown's fiction is Arthur Kimball's invaluable *Rational Fictions: A Study of Charles Brockden Brown* (McMinnville, Ore., 1968). Kimball develops his argument much more briefly in his article, "Savages and Savagism: Brockden Brown's Dramatic Irony," *Studies in Romanticism*, 6 (1967), 214-15.

[4]All parenthetical page references to *Wieland* are to the edition of Fred Lewis Pattee, *Wieland, or The Transformation, together with Memoirs of Carwin, the Biloquist, A Fragment* (New York, 1926).

Well into the nineteenth century it was the consensus of American critics, ministers and moralists that novels were at best frivolous and usually dangerous. Such hostility toward fiction was hardly unique to America, but it was particularly virulent in a new nation whose beginnings were in Puritanism and whose accepted official philosophy derived from the ethical realism of the Scottish Common Sense School.[5] Thus the Rev. Samuel Miller, whom Brown knew as a member of the New York Friendly Club, complained in 1803 that novel-reading had "a tendency too much to engross the mind, to fill it with artificial views, and to diminish the taste for more solid reading." "To fill the mind with unreal and delusive pictures of life," he claimed, "is, in the end, to beguile it from sober duty, and to cheat it of substantial enjoyment."[6] Miller's attack is thoroughly representative. And behind such attacks there lay, as Terence Martin has observed, "a predisposition of the American mind to be suspicious of imaginative experience." The attacks on the novel, Martin writes, were "based ultimately...on the primary metaphysical principle that the order of possibility is delusive, distorted and dangerous."[7]

Confirmation of this principle was not hard to find; one had to look no farther than Hugh Blair's *Lectures on Rhetoric and Belles Lettres* (1783), whose influence on official American thought was omnipresent and for which Brown expressed admiration as early as 1787.[8] Imaginative literature, according to Blair's *Rhetoric,* is more characteristic of primitive than of modern societies: "The imagination is most vigorous and predominant in youth; with

[5]Attitudes toward fiction in early America are discussed in G. Harrison Orians, "Censure of Fiction in American Romances and Magazines, 1789-1810," *PMLA,* 52 (1937), 195-214; in William Charvat's chapter on "Criticism and Fiction" in *The Origins of American Critical Thought 1810-1835* (Philadelphia, 1936), pp. 134-63; and especially in Terence Martin's *The Instructed Vision: Scottish Common Sense Philosophy and the Origins of American Fiction* (Bloomington, Ind., 1961).

[6]*A Brief Retrospect of the Eighteenth Century* (New York, 1803), II, 179, 176.

[7]*The Instructed Vision,* pp. 54, 76.

[8]Brown's mention of Blair occurs in an address given at the opening meeting of the Belles Lettres Society, a group of young Philadelphia law students devoted to the discussion of philosophy and literature. (Reprinted in William Dunlap, *The Life of Charles Brockden Brown* [Philadelphia, 1815], II, 27.) On the influence of Blair's *Rhetoric* in America see Martin's *The Instructed Vision* and Charvat's *Origins of American Critical Thought.*

advancing years, the imagination cools, and the understanding ripens." Imagination partakes, therefore, of the other salient quality of youth and barbarism: "In the infancy of all societies, men are much under the dominion of imagination and passion." *Imagination and passion:* this equation, which Blair could simply assume in 1783, explains the alarm of Samuel Miller and his fellow moralists. "Poetry," in Blair's definition, is "the language of passion, or of enlivened imagination."[9] "Understanding" is the cement of a settled society. Since "passion" is foe to both, so too is "imagination." It is no coincidence that Blair associated imagination with that very state of society to which Rousseau and his followers appealed for the sanction of their revolutionary doctrines. As Martin puts it: "The world of the imagination thus became in a special way a region of terror. ... In the United States, with the imagination regarded as a threat to society, the terror took on a new and local dimension."[10]

Most contemporary novelists, oddly enough, shared this fear of fiction and imagination. Following the logic of Blair's equation such writers as William Hill Brown turned the seduction novel's warning against the triumph of passion into the critic's warning against the dangers of novel-reading. In a long footnote to *The Power of Sympathy* (1789) Brown draws a clear moral from the seduction of Elizabeth Whitman, a woman possessed of "a poetical imagination." "She was a great reader of novels and romances," he writes, "and having imbibed her ideas of the *characters of men,* from these fallacious sources, became vain and coquettish, and rejected several offers of marriage, in expectation of receiving one more agreeable to her fanciful idea."[11] Miss Whitman, illustrating Brown's logic, is seduced by novel-reading.

The same logic dominates the writings of Charles Brockden Brown. In 1798 he published a story, "A Lesson on Sensibility," which tells of one Archibald, "a youth of lively parts," but one whose "sensibility had become diseased by an assiduous study of those Romancers and Poets, who make love the basis of their fictions." Through a process too involved to relate here, his

[9]*Lectures on Rhetoric and Belles Lettres* (Philadelphia, 1844), pp. 72, 66, 421.
[10]*The Instructed Vision*, p. 107.
[11]*The Power of Sympathy,* William S. Kable, ed. (Columbus, 1969), pp. 33, 32n-33n.

diseased sensibility leads to a rather gruesome disappointment in love (involving the premature burial and starvation of his beloved), and Archibald is converted into a raving maniac. "He has remained for some years," the narrator moralizes, "an example of the fatal effects of addicting the undisciplined mind to books, in which Nature is so fantastically and egregiously belied."[12] The point is made even more clearly in the revised version of the story published in 1809 in Joseph Dennie's *Port Folio* as "Insanity: A Fragment." In this version the narrator's husband intrudes at the close to reveal that the experience to which Archibald attributes his insanity never happened, but derived solely from the effect of books on his sensibility, "that the whole existed only in his own imagination:...that the whole is a dream, regarded by him indeed as unquestionable reality, but having not the slightest foundation in truth."[13] Such, for Brown, were the dangers of exposing the mind to unreal and delusive pictures of life.

The same dangers lie behind the disastrous events of *Wieland,* which also culminates in insanity. At the close of her story, still believing that Carwin's ventriloquism produced Theodore's supernatural voices, Clara moralizes: "If Wieland had framed juster notions of moral duty, and of the divine attributes; or if I had been gifted with ordinary equanimity or foresight, the double-tongued deceiver would have been baffled and repelled." (273) Carwin is only indirectly responsible for Wieland's madness. His vocal deceptions only unsettle Theodore's ability to distinguish between fact and fiction, leading him to accept the reality of voices produced by his own imagination. But this is precisely the sense in which moralists, including Brown, feared that fiction would unsettle the mental balance of novel-readers.

And there is much else in Brown's novel to link Carwin's ventriloquism with the art of the novelist. Early in 1798 Brown wrote that the purpose of the novelist's "lofty eloquence" is to

[12] Philadelphia *Weekly Magazine,* 2 (1798), 71, 72.

[13] *Port Folio,* 3rd Series, 1 (1809), 168. For the relationship between these two stories, and for the evidence that they were written by Brown, see Robert Hemenway, "Brockden Brown's Twice-Told Insanity Tale," *American Literature,* 40 (1968), 211-15.

"enchain the attention and ravish the souls of those who study and reflect."[14] On first meeting Carwin, Clara has an almost sexual reaction to the power of his voice:

> The voice was not only mellifluent and clear, but the emphasis was so just, and the modulation so impassioned, that it seemed as if an heart of stone could not fail of being moved by it. It imparted to me an emotion altogether involuntary and incontroulable. When he uttered the words, "for charity's sweet sake," I dropped the cloth that I held in my hand, my heart overflowed with sympathy and my eyes with unbidden tears. (59)

Here is the writer's passionate eloquence, uncontrollable in its appeal, irrational in its effects. Clara is "ravished" by its power. And Carwin is also a teller of tales, a literary artist. "His narratives," Clara writes, "were constructed with so much skill, and rehearsed with so much energy, that all the effects of a dramatic exhibition were frequently produced by them." (84)

Carwin is a special sort of artist. Clara assures us repeatedly that her own tale is true, that she is disguising nothing. Not so with Carwin: "His tale is a lie, and his nature devilish." (243) "It would be vain," Clara is told by her suspicious lover, Pleyel, "to call upon Carwin for an avowal of his deeds. It was better to know nothing, than to be deceived by an artful tale." (145) In Clara's contest with Carwin, then, the conflict between sincerity and duplicity acquires a specifically literary dimension. In *The Rhapsodist* (1789), his first important literary production, Brown had his persona insist on the ideal of absolute literary truthfulness: "I intend that the sincerity of my character shall be the principal characteristic of these papers. ... I speak seriously, when I affirm that no situation whatsoever will justify a man in uttering a falsehood." And yet even the Rhapsodist feared that his literary performance might be considered "as an artful contrivance, designed to show the skill and ingenuity, rather than the fidelity, of the

---

[14]"Advertisement for *Sky Walk*" (a novel completed but never published) in Harry R. Warfel, ed., *The Rhapsodist and Other Uncollected Writings by Charles Brockden Brown* (New York, 1943), p. 136.

author's pencil."[15] If Clara represents the Rhapsodist's ideal of absolute literary sincerity, then Carwin represents his fear that all literary expression, being "artful," leads inevitably to artificiality and deception.

Such fears were elaborated in 1800 in a series of essays, entitled *The Speculatist,* probably written by Brown. In one of these essays a friend of the Speculatist wonders whether even the man of benevolent sincerity may be but "performing a part in order to obtain [the world's] good opinion." If so, the friend concludes, "life appears like one great masquerade, at which every object is decked in false colours, and the attention of observers diverted from an useful analysis of the genuine character, by the vagaries of the one which is assumed."[16] It is fitting that Carwin's eloquence should find its ultimate expression in ventriloquism, vocal masquerade.

An essayist in Brown's *Literary Magazine* wrote in 1803 that the artist gains his ends, "not by imitating the works of nature, but by assuming her power."[17] Such ideas particularly alarmed contemporary critics of fiction, who ultimately rested their case against imagination on the contention that the artist in his manipulations of reality usurps the power of God.[18] Clara declares to the "double-

[15]Warfel, ed., *The Rhapsodist,* pp. 1, 9. *The Rhapsodist* reveals that for Brown, even at the very beginning of his career, sincerity was problematic on the various levels described by Henri Peyre: "aesthetic (Does language necessarily betray? Does technique imply artifice and distortion?); psychological (Does sincerity to oneself ever penetrate into all that, in ourselves, lies hidden from us, impervious to analytical probing?); social (Is our social self to be slighted? Or do truth to others and the commitment of the author to wider groups constitute higher duties than those to ourselves?...)" *(Literature and Sincerity* [New Haven, 1963], pp. 306-07). Behind all these problems, according to Peyre, lies the central question: "Can literature be sincere?" *(Ibid.,* p. 306). In addition to this question, however, Brown was troubled by a prior one: *should* literature be sincere?

[16]*The Monthly Magazine and American Review,* 3 (1800), 161-62. Brown edited *The Monthly Magazine* from 1799 to 1800, and apparently wrote much of the material (generally unattributed) that appeared in it. Professor Clark concludes that although "Brown's authorship of the *Speculatist* is uncertain...it is reasonably safe to assign these essays to his pen" *(Charles Brockden Brown,* p. 142n).

[17]*The Literary Magazine and American Register* (which Brown edited from 1803 to 1807), 1 (1803), 150.

[18]On this point see Martin, *The Instructed Vision,* pp. 61-63.

tongued deceiver": "Thou art the author of these horrors!...I adjure thee, by that God whose voice thou hast dared to counterfeit, to save my life!" (255) Carwin, *"author* of these horrors," masquerades as God. In so doing he sets forward a chain of circumstances leading to Wieland's illusory visions of divinity.

At the close Clara assures us that Carwin "saw, when too late, the danger of imposture." (267) She claims herself to have avoided this danger by adhering to an art based on sincerity. Yet when Theodore's imaginary voices turn him against her, Clara appeals to the imposter Carwin to save her. He does so by counterfeiting the divine voice which has urged Wieland on, and by having that voice attest to the "truth" of its own non-existence. This conclusion is doubly ironic. To communicate the *truth* Carwin must resort to *imposture.* And his "truth" destroys Wieland just as surely as illusion destroyed Wieland's wife and children. "Now finally restored to the perception of truth," writes Clara, "...Wieland was transformed at once into the *man of sorrows!"* (258) Sincerity is once again corrupted by "artful" duplicity. Clara's true story has been opposed all along to Carwin's imposture. At the end, however, she can only declare to her remembered brother, who has committed suicide in his despair: "Oh that thy phrenzy had never been cured! that thy madness, with its blissful visions, would return!" (259) Even Clara turns at last from "truth" to the "blissful vision" of imagination and insanity. Her antifictional sincerity finally collapses under the weight of moral and artistic confusion.

The same confusion permeates the world of *Ormond* (1799). Constantia Dudley, another figure of sincerity and virtue, confronts the trials of poverty, of pestilence and ultimately of the villainous advances of Ormond, who announces at their first interview: "I will put your sincerity to the test." (128)[19] Ormond is Brown's fullest representation of the descent from idealism to villainy. He rigidly separates his high ideals from his practical actions. He is also, of all Brown's characters, the most sexually aggressive and the most clearly linked to the ideals and excesses of the French Revolution. All of these forces—depraved idealism, sexual passion and political radicalism—are brought to bear

[19]All parenthetical page references to *Ormond* are to the edition of Ernest Marchand, *Ormond* (New York, 1962).

against Constantia's virtue, against both her virginity and the ideals by which she tries to live. But Ormond has another attribute which seems inexplicable in terms of his function in the novel. "In early youth," writes the narrator, Sophia Courtland, "he discovered in himself a remarkable facility in imitating the voice and gestures of others." (95) We are told at some length the steps by which this facility became habitual. And yet after his first visit to Constantia disguised as a chimney-sweep, Ormond's love of disguise, so elaborately introduced, has no function in the plot.

On a symbolic level, however, his "remarkable facility" is quite appropriate. His abilities, we are told, "would have rendered his career, in the theatrical profession, illustrious." (95) Sophia writes that he "blended in his own person the functions of poet and actor, and his dramas were not fictitious but real." For Ormond the goal of such "real" drama is power: "Ormond aspired to nothing more ardently than to hold the reins of opinion—to exercise absolute power over the conduct of others, not by constraining their limbs or by exacting obedience to his authority, but in a way of which his subjects should be scarcely conscious." (147) It is in this sense that his "remarkable facility" is turned on Constantia: "By explaining his plans, opportunity was furnished to lead and to confine her meditations to the desirable track. By adding fictitious embellishments, he adapted it with more exactness to this purpose. By piecemeal and imperfect disclosures her curiosity was kept alive." (147) In 1798 Brown had characterized the novel as "a contexture of facts capable of suspending the faculties of every soul in curiosity."[20] Like Carwin, then, Ormond acts in a sense as a figure of the artist as master of duplicity.

Half way through *Ormond* Sophia introduces her title character, and begins by confessing her difficulties:

> I know no task more arduous than a just delineation of the character of Ormond. To scrutinize and ascertain our own principles are abundantly difficult. To exhibit those principles to the world with absolute sincerity can scarcely be expected. We are prompted to conceal and to feign by a thousand motives; but truly to portray the motives and relate the actions of another appears utterly impossible. (92)

[20]"Advertisement for *Sky Walk*,"Warfel, ed., *The Rhapsodist,* p. 136.

Sophia's confession indicates that for Brown the problem of fictional portrayal of character was analogous to the more general problem of literary sincerity. Both presented the writer with the difficulties of knowing and expressing the truth. In presenting himself, or in presenting the motives of another character, the writer was tempted into artfulness. And since he could only establish patterns of motivation through conjecture, he was forced to rely on imagination. In an 1800 essay, "The Difference between History and Romance," Brown identified the novelist's analysis of motive with "romance," with fiction.[21] And a few months after publishing *Ormond* he admitted the difficulty of such reliance on conjecture: "No situation can be imagined perfectly similar to that of an actual being."[22] Thus in spite of her prefatory claim that Ormond "is not a creature of fancy" (3), Sophia is finally forced to admit that her portrayal of him is nonetheless a work of imagination.

What happens in Sophia's story is that the imaginary quality of her *delineation* of Ormond becomes embodied in the character of Ormond as he acts in the novel. In 1798 Brown wrote that the writer's "eloquence" finds its fit object in "the man of soaring passions and intellectual energy."[23] In Brown's novels this man emerges, again and again, as not only the object but the objective correlative of this eloquent "energy" and of its terrors. In *The Rhapsodist* and in his portrayal of Carwin, Brown reveals his fear that such energy will be falsified by the effort to communicate it. The outcome of *Ormond* suggests that he feared equally what would happen if such communication were successful. Toward the close Ormond begins to abandon his habit of imposture. "The veil that shrouded this formidable being," writes Sophia, "was lifted high enough to make him be regarded with inexplicable horror." (231) She writes of Ormond, already associated with revolutionary violence, that "that in which he chiefly placed his boast was his sincerity." (94) Hugh Blair equated imagination with passion, and implied that both threatened society. In his final interview with Constantia, Ormond, figure of revolutionary sin-

[21]*Monthly Magazine*, 2 (1800), 251-53.

[22]"Walstein's School of History," in Warfel, ed., *The Rhapsodist,* p. 154.

[23]"Advertisement for *Sky Walk,*"Warfel, ed., *The Rhapsodist,* p. 136.

cerity and of the novelist's power, is transformed into the conventional villain of the seduction novel. All else failing, he determines to rape his fair antagonist. He thus reveals the purpose, the energy, at the heart of his elaborate masquerade: "My avowals of love were sincere; my passion was vehement and undisguised." (233) Confronted with this figure of vehement sincerity Constantia has no choice; she kills him.

Carwin and Ormond, men "of soaring passions and intellectual energy," become at last figures of the artist, trapped between sincerity and imposture, between literary energy, and the artfulness of literary order. To say this is not to reduce Brown's first two novels to the status of allegorical portraits of the artist. Rather in these novels the artistic conflict between sincerity and duplicity emerges as only one aspect of a more general opposition—literary, psychological and political—between energy and order. Brown's villains are *at the same time* seducers, revolutionaries and artists. As such they embody a whole complex of related forces allied against eighteenth-century ideas of stability. Brown was hardly original in perceiving the similarity between that passion which overthrows the understanding and those revolutionary doctrines which threaten to overthrow settled governments. Nor was he unique in perceiving the relationship of such revolutionary passion to the artistic imagination. In fact in portraying these forces acting in concert Brown was only expressing, in fictional form, the conventional wisdom of his age. Blair assumed the equation of imagination with passion. And there was clearly a close intellectual relationship between the conservative American fear of fiction and the contemporary fear of the spread of the French Revolution.

What makes Brown fascinating is the self-consciousness with which he made the conventional fear of fiction a central preoccupation of *works of fiction.* In this self-consciousness he seems quite modern. Carwin and Ormond threaten the order not only of the mind and the community but of the work of art as well. If they represent the disastrous practical consequences of the doctrines of sincerity by which Clara and Constantia attempt to live, they also represent the hazards of that literary sincerity by which Brown was attempting to write. In the horrible consequences of their impostures, and in their own precipitate descents from sincerity to masquerade, they express Brown's fears about the truth and the effects of fiction. In *Wieland* and *Ormond* such fears are embodied mainly in the figures of the villains. In *Edgar Huntly* and *Arthur Mervyn* they are embodied, as well, in the narrative structures of the novels.

In *Edgar Huntly* (1799) Brown is concerned neither with revolution nor with the inevitable descent from sincerity to deliberate imposture. As the narrator of his own tale, however, Edgar *is* concerned with the conflict between literary energy and literary order. He believes in the need for "order and coherence" in narrative and yet fears that such coherence may be irreconcilable with the emotional "truth" of his adventures: "Time may take away these headlong energies, and give me back my ancient sobriety; but this change will only be effected by weakening my remembrance of these events. In proportion as I gain power over words, shall I lose dominion over sentiments." (5)[24] This problem is central to Edgar's narrative. His story turns on the implications of telling and hearing tales, and on the ways in which rational forms of order ("words") obscure or repress the irrational sources of artistic energy ("sentiments"). In the narrative structure of *Edgar Huntly* Brown explores the means by which certain kinds of literary response attempt to reverse or overcome the revolutionary impulses revealed in *Wieland* and *Ormond*.

At the beginning of his story Edgar is seeking the murderer of his friend Waldegrave. He comes to suspect a mysterious somnambulist, Clithero Edny, and follows him into the wilderness to extort a confession. When Clithero does confess, however, it is to a quite different crime. *His* story, nested within Edgar's, tells of his having been raised by a Mrs. Lorimer, a benevolent woman persecuted by her villainous brother, Arthur Wiatte. In spite of Wiatte's treachery Mrs. Lorimer was convinced that her own survival depended on his continued existence. One night Clithero killed a thief in self defense, and then discovered to his horror that the assailant was Wiatte. Overwhelmed by guilt, in spite of his blameless motives, Clithero succumbed to an irrational compul-

[24]All parenthetical page references to *Edgar Huntly* are to *Edgar Huntly, or Memoirs of a Sleep-Walker* (Philadelphia, 1887).

sion to "save" Mrs. Lorimer from knowledge of her brother's death by killing her, too. His attempt failed, but she collapsed from shock, and Clithero fled convinced that his actions led to her death. Tormented by his "inexpiable guilt" he has come to the American wilderness.

As soon as he finishes his tale, which occupies six chapters of Brown's novel, Clithero vanishes into the forest. Edgar is deeply impressed by what he has heard. "I had communed," he writes, "with romancers and historians, but the impression made upon me by this incident was unexampled in my experience." (86-87) From here on the novel's action turns on Edgar's response to Clithero's narrative. Consciously, he is filled with compassion, with a sympathy that overwhelms moral judgment—which is to say that on the conscious level he reacts to Clithero's story like a good reader of sentimental fiction, substituting charity for censure. He sets out to exonerate Clithero and thus to "save" him. "It must at least be said," he argues, "that his will was not concerned in this transaction. He acted in obedience to an impulse which he could not control or resist. Shall we impute guilt where there is no design?" (87) The rational judgment of irrational behavior is that only a deliberate, rational act of the will can lead to the imputation of guilt.

Unconsciously, however, Edgar reacts to Clithero's story with a very different sort of sympathy. "My judgment," he writes, "was, for a time, sunk into imbecility and confusion. My mind was full of the images unavoidably suggested by this tale, but they existed in a kind of chaos." (87) Just as Clithero acted against Mrs. Lorimer "in obedience to an impulse which he could not control nor resist," and just as Clara Wieland's reaction to Carwin's voice was altogether involuntary and incontroulable" (59), so Edgar is propelled "unavoidably" into "a kind of chaos." Even as he consciously dismisses the importance of Clithero's irrational behavior, he unconsciously begins to imitate it. He is himself transformed into a somnambulist, thereby manifesting a guilt in some obscure way comparable to Clithero's. He follows Clithero into a wilderness clearly symbolic of the unconscious mind.[25] And his new life,

[25]On Brown's use of landscape in *Edgar Huntly* for the purpose of psychological symbolism see Kenneth Bernard, "Charles Brockden Brown and the Sublime," *The Personalist,* 45 (1964), 235-49; and Paul Witherington, "Image and Idea in

described as a "hideous dream," becomes at last quite literally dreamlike. After retiring to sleep in his uncle's house he awakens in a cave, from which he emerges to battle Indians and panthers and to make hundred-foot leaps into the Delaware River. As he notes himself, these fantastic adventures must seem to the reader "the vision of fancy, rather than the lesson of truth." (185)

Edgar's response to Clithero's story hints at a profound unconscious sympathy between artist and audience. Many details both of the story and of Edgar's response to it hint further at the mechanism by which such irrational sympathy operates. For instance Clithero notes, almost casually, of his murder of Wiatte: "I was impelled by an unconscious necessity. Had the assailant been my father, the consequence would have been the same." (70) Edgar pursues, and yet becomes curiously identified with, Indians who years before killed *his* father. He uses a rifle given to him by his paternal teacher, Saresfield. At the beginning of his dream-adventure he finds this rifle in the possession of one of his Indian victims; he learns later that it had just been used to kill his uncle, who adopted him after his father's death. And near the close he "unwittingly" turns this rifle on his last remaining father-figure, Saresfield, who had given him the weapon in the first place. Both Edgar and Clithero, it would seem, are plagued by unconscious urges to slay figures of paternal authority, and by the "irrational" guilt consequent to these urges. They even have a "father" in common: Saresfield turns out to be Mrs. Lorimer's long-lost fiancé. Thus it is small wonder that Edgar reacts so powerfully to Clithero's strange tale. It reveals, symbolically, his own repressed dreams and impulses.

The oedipal patterns in Clithero's and Edgar's stories, only sketched here, are quite blatant to the modern reader. One can only speculate about Brown's awareness and intention in portraying such patterns. What *is* clear, though, is that in the course of the novel irrational motivation and identification, whatever their source, triumph over the rational sympathy with which Edgar

---

Wieland and *Edgar Huntly," The Serif,* 3, No. 4 (Dec. 1966), 19-26. For a more general discussion of the psychological dimensions of *Edgar Huntly,* and of Brown's fiction as a whole, see Chapter 5, "Charles Brockden Brown and the Invention of the American Gothic," in Leslie Fiedler's *Love and Death in the American Novel* (Cleveland, 1962).

attempts to control his response to Clithero's story. This is the essential action of *Edgar Huntly*. Rational sympathy (the "charity" of sentimental fiction) is undercut by unconscious sympathy. At the end of the novel, having fortunately missed his shot at Saresfield, and having emerged from his own wilderness of guilt, Edgar tries to work out a similar deliverance for Clithero. He rushes into the wilderness to tell him that Mrs. Lorimer is not dead after all, but married to Saresfield and living in New York. "I come," he announces, "to outroot a fatal but powerful illusion." (275) His information has, however, precisely the contrary effect from what he intends. He simply reawakens Clithero's compulsion to murder his benefactress, driving him to New York where he is arrested and where he commits suicide on the way to an asylum.

Edgar has maintained throughout that "the magic of sympathy, the perseverance of benevolence, though silent, might work a gradual and secret revolution, and better thoughts might insensibly displace those desperate suggestions which now governed [Clithero]." (107) At the close he finally agrees with Saresfield that Clithero's "understanding" has been "utterly subverted" (277), making him immune to the workings of benevolence. But Edgar never makes the final step; he never consciously understands the implications of Clithero's insanity for his own and Clithero's narratives, and for narrative in general. He is never willing or able to admit, even to himself, that the appeal of Clithero's tale, the "magic" of its "sympathy," derived not from "better thoughts" but from the "desperate suggestions" at its heart. Edgar thus pulls back from the fullest implications of his own story. If Brown's novel records the undercutting of charity by compulsion, of "better thoughts" by "desperate suggestions," it does so only through narrative irony. Overtly, in Edgar's account, "words" do finally triumph over "sentiments."

The protagonist of Brown's fourth novel even more persistently submerges "desperate suggestions" beneath "better thoughts." *Arthur Mervyn* was published in two parts. The first appeared early in 1799, before *Edgar Huntly*. Part two was given to the printer early in 1800. The first part is very much in the manner of *Wieland* and *Ormond*. A sincere protagonist, this time a young man from the country, enters an alien city-world dominated by "perils and deceptions." (43)[26] Like Constantia Dudley he confronts the smallpox epidemic of 1793. And he encounters an older man whose character is strongly reminiscent of Carwin and Ormond. Welbeck's villainy has mainly to do with sexual licentiousness and financial fraud, but it is also associated with literature. "My ambition," he declares, "has panted, with equal avidity, after the reputation of literature and opulence." (95) He thus assumes familiar poses of the artist-figure in Brown's fiction: as forger, and as vocal imposter counterfeiting the voices of others. In the relationship of Arthur with Welbeck, then, we have the familiar contest between sincerity and duplicity. As Arthur is physically wasted by fever, so his reputation is blasted by his association with Welbeck. He is saved at the end only through the charity of a Dr. Stevens, to whom he tells his story, and whose own voice frames the narrative of the first part.

In part two Arthur's adventures take a different direction. Sincerity and virtue triumph. Welbeck dies repentant. Through an almost obsessive course of benevolence Arthur rescues his reputation, rising into circles of affluence and finally marrying a rich widow. He does all this by insisting on absolute sincerity of conduct. Even his view of the city changes. Wider experience of Philadelphia convinces him "that if cities are the chosen seats of misery and vice, they are likewise the soil of all the laudable and strenuous productions of mind." (280) Part one's vision of evil is transformed, in part two, into a vision of opportunity.

Part two also transforms the earlier treatment of literary truth and deception. In part one Welbeck's inveterate imposture is contrasted with Arthur's insistent honesty—just as, in *Wieland*, Carwin's duplicity is contrasted with Clara's sincerity. In part two Welbeck's importance subsides, and it is Arthur himself who comes under suspicion of fraud. In fact part two functions as a sort of commentary on the narrative Arthur presents in part one. It begins with the efforts of Dr. Stevens' friends to convince him of the falsehood of Arthur's tale. One merchant argues, as Stevens writes:

[26]All parenthetical page references to *Arthur Mervyn* are to the edition of Warner Berthoff, *Arthur Mervyn: or Memoirs of the Year 1793* (New York, 1962).

that Mervyn was a wily imposter; that he had been trained in the
arts of fraud, under an accomplished teacher; that the tale which
he had told to me, was a tissue of ingenious and plausible lies; that
the mere assertions, however plausible and solemn, of one like him,
whose conduct had incurred such strong suspicions, were unworthy
of the least credit. (215)

The action of part two turns mainly on the question of whether or
not Arthur will be able to prove his sincerity against such
aspersions.

Arthur's problem recalls that of Godwin's Caleb Williams.[27]
Like Caleb he has nothing to support his tale but the air of
sincerity with which he tells it. But there is an important difference of emphasis in *Arthur Mervyn.* Godwin's concern with
Caleb's predicament—with his inability to disprove the false
accusations of Falkland—is almost entirely social and psychological. He is concerned with the possibility of justice in a legal
system based on corroborative evidence, and with the psychological consequences of Caleb's exposure of Falkland. For Brown
what is at stake is not justice in society but belief in truth as an
abstract ideal. "If Mervyn has deceived me," Stevens confesses to
one of his suspicious friends, "there is an end to my confidence
in human nature. All limits to dissimulation, and all distinctions
between vice and virtue will be effaced. No man's word, no force
of collateral evidence shall weigh with me an hair." (236-37)

And such confidence has a specifically literary dimension. By
shifting the narrative point of view from Arthur to Stevens, Brown
calls attention to the fact that Arthur's narrative *is* a narrative,
possibly a work of fiction. "Nothing but his own narrative," writes
the doctor, "repeated with that simple but nervous eloquence,
which we had witnessed, could rescue him from the most heinous
charges. . . . His tale could not be the fruit of invention; and yet,
what are the bounds of fraud? Nature has set no limits to the

---

[27]The influence of *Caleb Williams* (1794) on Brown's fiction, and particularly
on *Arthur Mervyn,* is quite evident and has received much comment. Dunlap
assures us that in the 1790's Brown "was an avowed admirer of Godwin's style,
and the effects of that admiration, may be discerned in many of his early compo-
sitions" *(Life, II, 15).* Describing a work in progress—"something in the form of a
romance"—in his journal in 1797 Brown referred to *Caleb Williams* as the standard by which such a work should be judged *(Ibid.,* I, 107).

combinations of fancy." (218) As Melville would do half a century later in *The Confidence-Man,* Brown in *Arthur Mervyn* links confidence in human nature with confidence in literary truth, and subjects both to powerful scrutiny. To believe in Arthur (or "author"?) one must trust the art, the "nervous eloquence," of his story.

The novel's comic conclusion seems to vindicate both Arthur and the possibility of sincerity in literature. Throughout the second part Arthur insists on the efficacy of telling the truth, "without artifice or disguise." (294) His sincerity is rewarded with the restored confidence of Stevens' skeptical friends. And yet the reader's skepticism, once aroused, is not so easily quieted. The very complexity of the novel's narrative structure raises doubts about the reliability of all narrative. And while one hardly suspects Arthur of the deliberate sort of fraud practiced by Welbeck, one cannot avoid the suspicion that he is at least deceiving himself.[28]

For one thing, his benevolent honesty often has quite disastrous consequences for others, as he himself acknowledges. "Good intentions," he admits, "unaided by knowledge, will, perhaps, produce more injury than benefit." Yet he insists that only conscious intention matters, whatever the result. "We must not be unactive because we are ignorant. Our good purposes must hurry to performance, whether our knowledge be greater or less." (309) This obliviousness is not, however, completely ingenuous. If Arthur ignores the hazardous consequences of his sincerity for others, he seldom forgets the possible beneficial consequences of that sincerity for himself. He always seems to have a *reason* for telling the truth. And the prosperity of the novel's conclusion suggests that virtue is to be regarded not as its own reward but as a particularly efficacious way to wealth. One recalls the friend's musings in the *Speculatist* essays, published four months after part two of *Arthur Mervyn* went to the printer—his suspicion

[28]On the question of the truthfulness of Arthur's narrative see especially Patrick Brancaccio, "Studied Ambiguities: *Arthur Mervyn* and the Problem of the Unreliable Narrator," *American Literature,* 42 (1970), 18-27. The novel's elaborate narrative structure is described in detail in Kenneth Bernard, *"Arthur Mervyn:* The Ordeal of Innocence," *Texas Studies in Literature and Language,* 6 (1965), 441-44.

that even the benevolent man is but "performing a part in order
to obtain [the world's] good opinion." Dr. Stevens, at the outset,
provides Arthur's adventures with a fitting motto. "Sincerity,"
he observes, "is always safest." (11)

If the reader has cause to suspect the motive behind Arthur's
sincerity of behavior he has even more cause to suspect the motive
behind his narrative. Arthur's story is offered as a didactic illustration of the triumph of virtue over vice, of benevolence over
corruption. Each confrontation with evil simply provides another
opportunity to display the corrective power of sincerity. Like
Edgar Huntly, with whom he also shares a belief in the supremacy
of the rational will, Arthur believes in the ability of "better
thoughts" to overcome "desperate suggestions," and this belief
functions as the moral of his tale. And yet such desperate suggestions emerge in spite of Arthur's conscious narrative purpose.
The sense of pestilential depravity pervading Philadelphia is
never quite washed away by the second part's comic momentum.
And Arthur's benevolent moral is undercut by his own story—
the story of a young man who idolizes his dead mother, loathes
his father (for having "victimized" her), and leaves home when
his father takes a second wife, a woman whose "superabundant
health" (16) disturbs Arthur. The suspicions of Dr. Stevens'
friends focus mainly on Arthur's account of his childhood and
youth. In their view Arthur simply rebelled against his father's
just authority. They have also heard, from other sources, that
Arthur has had sexual relations with his stepmother.

At the end of his story Arthur spurns the love of a beautiful
young woman in order to marry his heiress, Achsa Fielding, an
older widow to whom he repeatedly refers as "Mamma." Just
before their marriage he confesses to feeling a "nameless sort of
terror" (419) and has a dream in which Mrs. Fielding's first husband (presumably his "Papa") returns to kill him. This dream
suggests that Arthur's motives, for all his overt benevolence, are
not very different from those of Clithero Edny or Edgar Huntly.
The dream even induces in Arthur a brief bout of somnambulism.
What matters, though, is his utter rejection of the dream's implications, both psychological and literary—paralleling his earlier
rejection of the pestilential evil of Philadelphia. "I hate your

dream," says Achsa. "It is a horrid thought." "Why," replies Arthur, "you surely place no confidence in dreams." (429) If Arthur feels unconscious guilt for leaving his father and marrying his "Mamma," he refuses to admit it to the reader or to himself. On learning of his father's death he writes: "I was greatly shocked at this intelligence." But then "better thoughts" come to the fore. After some time, he writes, "my reason came to my aid, and shewed me that this was an event, on the whole, and on a disinterested and dispassionate view, not unfortunate." (376-77)

Many readers have noticed the irony of *Arthur Mervyn*, but they have generally been hesitant to give Brown full credit for it.[29] It would seem, however, that the book's irony is full, deliberate and devastating. Against Arthur's profession of virtuous intention stands his unacknowledged but persistent self-interestedness. Against the novel's apparent vindication of narrative sincerity stands the welter of suppressed motives revealed briefly in the final dream. In 1789 Brown's Rhapsodist wrote: "It is a very whimsical situation when a person is about to enter into company, and is at a loss what character or name to assume in it."[30] Arthur is the first of Brown's protagonists to "enter into company" with complete success, without agonizing over the question of what "name or character" to "assume." But he does not resolve the Rhapsodist's doubts; he simply suppresses them. He maintains his faith in social and literary order by averting his eyes from the dangerous psychological sources of literary energy and from the Rhapsodist's fear that all literary character is "assumed." Arthur turns sincerity on its head. He is a *pragmatic* idealist, wilfully ignoring all those aspects of his idealism and its consequences which terrified Brown's earlier protagonists. His trick, as a good American, is to act and write artificially without knowing it. He

[29]Warner Berthoff, for instance, writes that "the moral irony in the contrasts between the hero's priggish reflections on events and the melodrama of his actual career is remarkably consistent," but feels compelled to insist that "one does not wish to claim too much for Brown as a comic artist manqué, nor as an ironist" (Introduction to Berthoff, ed., *Arthur Mervyn*, p. xviii). James H. Justus gives Brown more credit in his excellent recent article, "Arthur Mervyn, American," *American Literature*, 42 (1970), 304-24.

[30]Warfel, ed., *The Rhapsodist*, p. 3.

completes the process begun by Edgar Huntly, who at least admitted that Clithero was immune to benevolent salvation. Arthur's earnestness is never daunted. But it is the earnestness, as Brown's irony makes clear, of the confidence-man.

Brown's first four novels, then, portray the complex collision of sincerity with duplicity on many levels—philosophical, political, psychological, literary. It is on this last level that they are most interesting to the student of later American fiction. Their importance is not mainly a matter of influence, although such writers as Cooper, Poe and Hawthorne knew Brown's work.[31] Rather they are interesting because they show how the intellectual and literary climate of America led an early novelist toward preoccupations which would characterize the best American fiction of the next sixty years and beyond. Such critics as Charles Feidelson, Richard Chase and Leslie Fiedler have found in the American novel such distinctive qualities as pervasive psychological symbolism, intense self-consciousness about literary form and formal reliance on extreme and abstract conflicts and oppositions. They have also explored, in various ways, the relationship of such literary qualities to more general social and intellectual patterns in American culture.[32] What Brown's example demonstrates is the relationship of such literary qualities to the specific predicament of an author trying to write fiction in America.

The divergence of American fiction from British has long

[31]In his original preface to *The Spy* (1821) Cooper referred disparagingly to the cave scene in *Edgar Huntly,* containing "an American, a savage, a wild cat, and a tomahawk, in a conjunction that never did, nor ever will occur" (Reprinted in *The Spy,* J. E. Morpurgo, ed. [London, 1968], p. 1). Poe and Hawthorne were kinder. The former, in a review of Cooper's *Wyandotté,* distinguished between "popular" writers, such as Cooper, and writers of "more worthy and more artistical fictions." In the latter category he included Brown along with John Neal, William Gilmore Simms and Nathaniel Hawthorne (*The Works of Edgar Allan Poe,* Edmund Clarence Stedman and George Edward Woodberry, eds., 10 vols. [New York, 1914], VII, 4-5). In "The Hall of Fantasy," after discovering Fielding, Richardson and Scott on "conspicuous pedestals," Hawthorne writes: "In an obscure and shadowy niche was deposited the bust of our countryman, the author of Arthur Mervyn" (*Mosses from an Old Manse* [Boston, 1882], p. 198).

[32]See Charles Feidelson, Jr., *Symbolism and American Literature* (Chicago, 1953); Richard Chase, *The American Novel and Its Tradition* (Garden City, N.Y., 1957); and Leslie Fiedler, *Love and Death in the American Novel.*

been recognized. The tradition of Fielding, Austen, Scott and Eliot, whatever the great differences between these writers, presents a world of social reality, controlled by an author whose wisdom and fairness qualify him for the trust of his audience. It is generally supposed that the failure of American fiction to take such a course results from such things as the lack of intelligible social reality in America, the abstract nature of American intellectual culture, the enduring Puritan habit of introversion or the prevailing symbolic bias of the American imagination. All of these factors, surely, played their part in forming our literature. But Brown's novels suggest that what was ultimately in question was not the sort of reality to be portrayed but the very act of portrayal. One reason social reality is generally absent in our fiction is that both readers and writers, whatever their views about the intelligibility of *society,* were predisposed to distrust fictional *reality.* Thus the novelist's attention was continually deflected from his world to his art. In Brown's novels political and social conflict are absorbed in the prior problem of artistic conflict. Social initiation, finally, becomes a kind of metaphor for the literary process. Behind the political and philosophical debates that inform the plots of Brown's novels one finds the Rhapsodist's question of what "character or name" an author could or should "assume" when "about to enter into company."

And thus, too, the sane controlling intelligence of the novelist is replaced by the figure of the artist as imposter, the "double-tongued deceiver." Brown turns from those forms in which a reliable narrator mediates between the audience and the world of the novel. He turns instead to the forms which pretend to authenticity and immediacy—letters, memoirs, confessions. And yet the paradoxical effect of this immediacy is to *subvert* authenticity, to bring narration into the action and thereby to raise questions about the novel's overt sincerity. All four novels reveal a basic fear, essentially similar to the fears of contemporary moralists, of both the illusoriness and the consequences of imaginative fiction. The novel's unreal and delusive picture of life unsettles the balance of the mind; and in so doing it releases that repressed psychological energy which threatens not only the order of society but also the order of fiction—of the narrative communication between author and audience. Deliberately writing just the sort of fiction men like Samuel Miller feared, and fearing it himself, Brown inevitably entangled himself in the strange relationship between narrative unreliability and irrational psychology. Whatever its overt adherence to moral order ("understanding," "charity," "better thoughts"), the novel ultimately probed and liberated the imagination ("passion," "unconscious necessity," "desperate suggestions").

This same configuration—fear or distrust of art, concern with irrational psychology, use of deceptive narrators—appears again and again in the fiction of Irving, Poe, Hawthorne and Melville. It is no coincidence that Brown, while he lacked the skill of these later writers, stumbled upon their central preoccupations and themes. In 1789 the Rhapsodist identified the new American literature with the cult of sincerity over calculation, truth over style, justice over social custom and habit. Sixty-one years later, in his famous review of Hawthorne's *Mosses from an Old Manse,* Melville still linked the literary genius of America with the doctrine of literary sincerity, "the great Art of Telling the Truth." "No American writer," he declared, "should write like an Englishman, or a Frenchman; let him write like a man, for then he will be sure to write like an American."[33] The Rhapsodist, Brown had written, "will write as he speaks, and converse with his reader not as an author, but as a man."[34]

Within two years of the Hawthorne review Melville recorded in *Pierre* his agonizing recognition that novels are unreliable, that "truth-tellers" are in fact confidence-men, that "like knavish cards, the leaves of all great books [are] covertly packed."[35] And even in the review of Hawthorne's *Mosses* he acknowledged the need to "insinuate" truth "craftily."[36] In the third and fourth *Rhapsodist* essays Brown introduced a "correspondent" whose sole function is to undermine the Rhapsodist's pose of sincerity by revealing its artificiality. "First appearances deceive me," he

[33]"Hawthorne and His *Mosses*" (1850), in Edmund Wilson, ed., *The Shock of Recognition* (New York, 1955), pp. 195, 194.

[34]Warfel, ed., *The Rhapsodist,* p. 5.

[35]*Pierre: or, The Ambiguities,* Henry A. Murray, ed. (New York, 1949), p. 399. Already in 1849, of course, Melville had registered a milder disillusionment with the reliability of books in the guidebook episode of *Redburn.*

[36]Wilson, ed., *The Shock of Recognition,* p. 193.

writes, "more specially in *an author* [Brown's italics], who speaks, as it were from behind a curtain." The Rhapsodist promised to address the reader "not as an author, but as a man." "Permit me," writes the correspondent, "to address you as an author."[37] Already in 1789, then, we have the vision of Brown's major novels, and of so much later American fiction. It is the vision the Speculatist would articulate eleven years later: "Life appears like one great masquerade, at which every object is decked in false colours."[38] This is also the vision Hawthorne would embody in 1852 in *The Blithedale Romance,* and Melville in 1857 in *The Confidence-Man.*

[37]Warfel, ed., *The Rhapsodist,* p. 18.
[38]*Monthly Magazine,* 3 (1800), 162.

The Image of America:
From Hermeneutics to Symbolism

by Sacvan Bercovitch

My thesis might be stated most bluntly as a tautology: what best defines the Americanness in the major works of American romanticism is their use of the image of America. The tautology seems to me worth exploring because it pertains as such only to American literature. The Germanness of the German romantics, for example is *not* defined by their use of the image of Germany; more important, the "image of America" here signifies a unique literary strategy. Mid-nineteenth-century American nationalism reflects the euphoria of the times, the millennial fervor that eventuates in the Panslavic Dream, or in the mission of France, or in the manifest destiny of German *Kultur*. In European romantic literature, as Meyer Abrams has shown, this political millennialism shifts rather rapidly towards a faith in "the apocalypse of the mind." Confronted with what they considered the failure of the French Revolution, the leading English and German romantics renounced "mass action" for "individual quietism," advocating "a total revolution of consciousness" through the "act of creative perception." The American strategy I refer to undertakes to unite both of these developments, national and spiritual. In effect, it yokes together the internal and the external Kingdom of God by asserting the simultaneity of a geographical locale, America, and a mode of vision. It is a strategy that interrelates the disparate processes of history, perception and regeneration within a distinctive collective-individual consciousness. Its roots lie in Puritan New England; and it manifests itself in the American Renaissance as hermeneutics transformed into symbolism.

Several examples suggest themselves at once, Hester Prynne differs in many ways from Emma Bovary, but in no way more strikingly than that by which she grows into an emblem of the country. The symbolic implications of the "A" she wears embrace art and nature, the social and the moral sphere; they coalesce at the novel's center and end, into a *historic* design—what Dimmesdale in the climactic scene calls the "glorious destiny of the newly-chosen people of the Lord." Or again, Emerson's notion of the scholar may be said to derive from contemporary Neoplatonist theory, until we recognize that it builds upon the fusion of divine selfhood and national self-realization: for the nation so conceived is not only a state of soul, like Blake's Albion, or only a metaphor for the evolution of the race (as in Schiller's *Aesthetic Education*), but first and last America, a local habitation about to "fill the postponed expectation of the world." Or once more, the tragedy of Pierre—child of nature, symbolist *in extremis,* questor for the absolute—echoes the works of Shelley and Novalis, among others. Yet surely Melville marks his hero unmistakably as a representative American in order that the novel's catastrophe may sound a forecast of *national* doom. To be sure, Melville's attitude contrasts with Hawthorne's ironic tone no less than with Emerson's cosmic optimism. But the configuration itself is the same. In all three cases, it takes its distinctive shape from a literal-prophetic outlook, which, like the wood that made up the *Pequod,* could only be American.

This movement of different imaginations toward the same image applies most dramatically to Thoreau, because of his relentless opposition to all national institutions. If at first he used his daily walk, as he tells us, to get the United States out of his head, he came to feel that the country interfered with his walk, that public affairs more and more impinged upon his private vision. Nonetheless, he often associated walking, figuratively, with the Westward expansion of the nation. Of course he meant thereby to translate the activity into that humanized, quintessentially romantic *itinerarum mentis*—into the "golden West" of the imagination. What is significant is that, in thus separating politics from the imagination, he also meant his walking to stand for a terrestial, collective *itinerarum Americanis*. When he speaks with pride of "the prevailing tendency of my countrymen," when he exults in the higher laws they may imbibe from the "grander," "more ethereal" frontier landscape, his avowed intention, for all his radical individualism, is to make "evident" the plan of history. He outlines this in general as a "journey" from the Fall through Babylon and Rome, "Odin and Christ to—America"; specifically, the journey includes the exodus across the Atlantic ("a Lethean stream over which we have had an opportunity to forget the Old World"), the founding of the long-prophesied second Eden, and the "illimitable holiness" of the greater paradise to come. Thoreau's westward walk, in sum, is as much a symbol of "mass action" as it is a gesture of "individual quietism." Equating the country's progress with the purpose of creation, he declares that the sun is "the Great Western Pioneer whom all the nations follow....Else to what end does the world go on, and why was America discovered?"

Three aspects of Thoreau's view of history seem to me especially remarkable. First, it was a commonplace of the age, accepted literally rather than as myth, by a wide variety of thinkers —Emerson for one, and the young Melville. Second, as an approach to the meaning of America it was part of the legacy of colonial Puritanism. Indeed, the very analogies Thoreau draws between the Atlantic and Lethe, between the New World mission and the "westering" sun, recur persistently from the Great Migration down through the Civil War. And more than that. They recur with exactly the dual import that Thoreau elicits from them: the ocean-crossing as a baptismal-cleansing writ large; the sun as herald of the dawning Age of the Spirit, in man's psyche and for all mankind. The third, most important aspect of Thoreau's view of history concerns its function as symbol. His "walking" in this regard divides into two literal levels, which open in turn into two modes of spiritual ascent: the private act flowers into the atemporal garden of the soul; the national action consummates the course of time. So considered, the two levels of meaning diverge as sharply from one another as do the two romantic eschatologies. Thoreau's strategy of reconciliation is predictable enough in retrospect. It consists in making the subject an *American* walker.

The roots of this dialectic, I have said, lie in seventeenth-century New England; more broadly, they suggest a vital link between Puritanism and romanticism. I must therefore ask your indulgence at this point for a long digression. In the interests of time, and with Thoreau's "walking" in mind, I will deal with the concept of rebirth only, as a hermeneutic approach which becomes secularized into the symbolic-romantic parallel between the discrete and the universal, the growth of a mind and the journey of mankind.

The preeminent English precursor is of course John Milton. As a Christian, he speaks of rebirth *christologically,* in terms of the life of faith; as a *Reformed* Christian, he views it *soteriologically,* in terms of the renascence of true Christianity after the long reign of Antichrist; as an *English* Reformed Christian, he uses it *providentially,* to describe the calling of a particular nation to lead the assault against the false church of Rome.[1] Christology and soteriology transpose the saint inwardly, and the elect historically, from a dead Babylon to New Jerusalem; as such, they form alternate individual and collective perspectives on the scheme of salvation. The concept of a social rebirth pertains to the secular sphere; as such, it connects soteriology with

---

[1] These divergent modes of Christian historiography may need a word of explanation. The *providential* view pertains to the course of secular history, the rise and fall of nations, communities, and individuals seen under the aspect of the *civitas terrena.* The historian tries to interpret these in terms of God's provisional judgments ("providences" as opposed to the pagan idea of "fortune"), in order to instruct his readers in matters of earthly welfare. The *soteriological* view pertains to the course of redemptive history, the ineluctable progress of the church, seen under the aspect of eternity, from the Old Testament Israel to the New Israel of Christ to the millennial reign of the saints. The historian "discovers" (or calculates) our place in this "divine scheme" by correlating the present state of the church with the promises and predictions of scripture. Bacon distinguishes between the two approaches as the History of Providence and the History of Prophecy. The latter was particularly important to the Reformers in rationalizing their break with the Catholic Church, which they identified, soteriologically, as the Antichrist described in the Book of Revelation. It became crucial to the English concept of elect nationhood; the New England Puritans went one step further and elevated America itself, as it were—past, present, and future—into the plan of redemptive history.

an entire people (saints and sinners alike), who have voluntarily bound themselves to an earthly endeavor, under a conditional "federal covenant." Milton affirmed the connection during the high tide of the Puritan Revolution, but only as a temporary, probational concurrence: no soldier in Cromwell's Army of Saints, he knew, could *ipso facto* claim regeneration, no English patriot could confuse his country *per se* with the Heavenly City, or his duties as Englishman with his prospects for eternity. Undoubtedly, this distinction between sainthood and statehood facilitated the Puritans' adjustment to mundane realities after the Restoration, as well as Milton's return to an exclusively inward eschatology of rebirth.

The case was otherwise in New Canaan. There, the body politic also constituted a gathering of the redeemed; there, as nowhere else, the saint prepared for salvation within a corporate historic undertaking destined to usher in the millennium. The reasons for this confluence of perspectives cannot be detailed here. Let it suffice to mention several factors that contributed to its uniqueness as hermeneutic. Theologically, as nonseparating congregationalists, the emigrants believed themselves bound both to the Invisible Universal Church *and* to the "indiscriminate," "impure" Protestant movement as a whole. Unlike the Separatists' church covenant, therefore, theirs entailed a federal errand no less than the search for perfection; and their errand, unlike the Presbyterians', enlisted them in the covenant of grace while engaging them in the political party of the future.

Experientially, their migration unveiled a pattern that profoundly enforced this double rationale. In the traditional allegory of rebirth, the saint flees the Egypt-Babylon of sin, crosses the Red Sea to salvation, perseveres through a desert of temptations, and so wins the celestial Canaan which by promise was already his. The parallels which the emigrants drew between these figural landmarks and their actual journey—from the European Babylon across the Atlantic Sea through the American wilderness—lent a special metaphoric dimension to their self-concept, one which joined their *vita nuova* as saints to the "newness" of the continent itself. Insofar as it had an Indian past, America was an ensign for them of the Devil's world, now at last to be reclaimed by Christ. What they considered its true identity they fashioned out of the end-time prophecies concerning the federally united remnant of the elect that would inherit the ends of the earth. In short, they named America by naming themselves. Other peoples, they explained, had their land by providence; they had it by promise. Thus separating the territory *qua* territory from its secular history, they imposed upon it a legendary past and an apocalyptic future which rendered its "true" inhabitants a "holy people," and its "discovery" a rebirth of mankind.

Seen in this light, America stands at the center of a configuration linking sacred and providential history in a daring synthesis. Bunyan's Christian may be traveling through England, but the nature of his pilgrimage lifts the story out of its immediate context; England is the wilderness as every postlapsarian country is the wilderness. Its landscape is significant to the conversion-crisis of any reader, in any place or period. The American wilderness gathered significance in just the opposite way: not in a process of deduction from a theological abstraction to an interior, psychological reality, but in a process of inference from physical reality to a metaphor of universal relevance. The more closely the settlers scrutinized their circumstances the more clearly they perceived in them a set of generalities which widened in concentric circles from fact to Christology to the scheme of redemption. As the single, separate Puritan related his rebirth in Christ to the Hebrew exodus, so the Puritans *en masse* interpreted their exodus as part of the divine plan. And what fused saint and society, traditional deduction and willed inference, was the idea of America. Or to put it in the terms I have applied to Thoreau: what yoked together the literal experience as it magnified the individual into Everyman with the literal enterprise as it revealed the renascence of mankind, was the heterogeneous image—composite of allegory and historiography but ultimately symbolic—of the *American* Puritan.

The development of seventeenth-century New England hermeneutics may be seen as a concerted effort to make the image work, both as rhetoric and as a method of self-definition. The problem of rhetoric solved itself, as it were, in the characteristically ambiguous terminology of exegesis, which made individual rebirth a *figura* of the rebirth of humanity, as in the journey to God by saint or church. But exegesis alone could not cope with the problem of self-definition. "Puritan" and "American" denoted respectively selfhood in Christ and tribal selfhood, and each of these entailed an independently comprehensive outlook. The Puritan outlook transmuted history into spiritual biography, as in *Pilgrim's Progress;* the American outlook located the individual within secular time, as in Milton's *History of Britain.* Hence their congruity demanded configuration by reality; and reality, in *its* characteristic way, resisted the alliance. Rhetorically, the clergy could use the concept of the "city on a hill" to mean at once a political community, a congregation of visible saints, a haven for the new-born soul, and a "specimen" of New Jerusalem. In reality, they found all too often that these meanings were *not* interchangeable. All too often membership in the church-state failed to confer dual citizenship in the City of God and in the City of Man. Even as the howling wilderness blossomed like the rose, their analysis of the errand itself increasingly jarred with the requisite ulterior significations. So it is that in the first generation their use of the image of America betrays a deep-seated tension between actuality and anticipation. So it is, too, that the image realizes its full potential for synthesis only toward the end of the century, with the theocracy's demise. What we are wont to shrug off as a "period of transition" is really a decisive moment in literary continuity. The discordances in the early writing convey the birth-pangs of the ill-fated Holy Commonwealth; the later rhetorical triumph—by which the founders' design became an enduring cultural legacy—testifies to the creative power of the imagination.

It was a triumph wrought from social defeat by recourse to the intrinsic subjectivity of the symbolic mode. Milton could abandon England to the way of the world because at bottom he had always dissociated his role in history from his status as Christian. The latter-day orthodoxy refused to abandon their concept of America because their self-definition was interwoven with their definition of the New World venture. Drawing out the implications of the emigrants' hermeneutics, they rejected temporal reality as the basis of American Puritan selfhood, and relocated their center of historic consciousness where perhaps (by virtue of its essentially symbolic nature) it should always have been, in the eye of the transcendental beholder. That is, the latter-day orthodoxy invested the tribal self with the prerogatives of spiritual biography. And if thereby they abstracted the "American" as a national figure into the realm of the absolute that seemed no more than just. "America," after all, was the land of promise, set apart from its neighbors by its special destiny, like Bunyan's Pilgrim. Their errand — in 1700 as in 1630 — meant not what it was as dead fact but how it appeared as the facts sprang to life under the aspect of Christology and soteriology.

In sum, the second- and third-generation ministers separated the false from the true America hermeneutically by separating them perceptually, as alternative views of the nation's tendency. One view focused on common providence, as though God's Country were no different from Italy or England, from Canada or Argentina. The other view, the true one, was centered in the mind journeying to God as it absorbed the American past and radiated the ineluctable American journey into the future. Microcosm became macrocosm: the country was not *like* its exemplary consciousness; it *was* that consciousness, or *(mutatis mutandis)* a collection of kindred consciousnesses, each of them recapitulating the exodus to America, each of them representing the country's "prevailing tendency," each of them foreshadowing the millennium at the end of the road — each of them, in Thoreau's words, refuting the literalist's here and now by embodying the symbolic "meeting of two eternities, past and future," that vindicated the national calling.

The image of America, then, as it grows out of Puritan thought, involves nothing less than a *Weltanschauung*. As the image withdraws further into the shelter of the regenerate consciousness, it reaches more omnivorously outward. The same strategy that protects it from reality compels it to embrace the course of history; and conversely, the same strategy that directs the symbolist to absorb the materials of history compels him to lift those materials out of history proper into the domain of the imagination. The relation between Milton and his romantic successors reveals a recurrent cycle, in which political engagement and renunciation is followed by the poet's affirmation of his interior vision. The relation between American Puritanism and American romanticism reveals a continuous spiral, unfolding through a proces-

sion of representative consciousnesses that increasingly enlarge
the symbolic framework of their collective-individual identity.
We can trace the development in the eighteenth century from
Cotton Mather, who wrote his self-justifying *Magnalia* to preserve the Puritan errand whether it "may live any where else or
no," to Jonathan Edwards, who felt that of all Americans he alone
understood the country's promise, through Timothy Dwight,
whose national epic is essentially an epic of the national poet.[2]

No doubt, the literary flowering of that outlook in the mid-
nineteenth century was stimulated by supportive elements in
romanticism: among others, Promethean individualism, heroic
alienation, and the doctrine of the protean creative imagination.
In this context, the representative American consciousness finds
its fullest poetic expression in Whitman's solitary singer — dis-
solving and reconstituting in himself, *as* himself, the geography,
history, prospects, and inhabitants of the New World — and its
finest fictional expression in our "romance" novels, with their
striking emphasis on typical persons at the expense of social
reality, even while they dwell obsessively on the meaning of
America. For the present purpose, it may be emblemized in
Thoreau's westward walk, as it leads toward what he calls "the
only true America." Implicit in his autobiographical supra-
personal journey is the giant inversion that shapes the parodistic
structure and language of *Walden:* its numerous references to
Franklinesque "economy," frontier life, the Puritan past, and
popular adaptations of the national dream, such as that exempli-
fied in the story of "poor John Field," the Irish immigrant who

[2]The persistence of this outlook owes much to the fact that the Puritan myth
also established itself in the society at large. This is not the place to examine
the nature of that relationship, nor to detail the reasons for the popular acceptance of the myth — though several factors may be noted in passing: for example,
the need prompted by successive waves of migration for a corporate identity
transcending the caprice of Providence; and the need of the westward movement
for a national purpose which would explain away the Indian rights to the land;
and more generally, the need to reverse colonial dependencies — political, economic, artistic — so that the United States *as* America might become at once heir
and teacher of the Old World. The Americans who spoke for the exemplary
national consciousness were responding to many of these needs, while alternately
(sometimes simultaneously) adopting and rejecting the social tendencies which
for their countrymen confirmed the American promise.

mistook America for the land of *economic* rebirth, and so was living "by some derivative old-country mode in this primitive new country." Clearly the "*new* country" Thoreau speaks of is America, actually as well as ideally, but it excludes the industrialized North and East, the slavery-infested South, the land-grabbing, Indian-massacring West. America *is* Thoreau, at Walden Pond or journeying west, the *true* pioneer, the *true* entrepreneur, the *true* descendant of the Puritans, in Alcott's words "the sole signer of the Declaration and a Revolution in himself"—and in himself, we may add, the *terminus ad quem* of the city on a hill.

"Poor John Field!" He "had rated it a gain," Thoreau laments, "in coming to America, that here you could get tea, and coffee, and meat every day." We almost feel ourselves at such moments (and Thoreau has many of them) in the presence of a seventeenth-century colonial Jeremiah decrying the idols of land and profit. But the early theocrats' tone is one of anxiety; the lamentation bespeaks their involvement in day-by-day exigencies as these were eroding the collective venture within which they defined their personal identity. Thoreau has no such anxiety. All we sense is his scorn for un-American institutions, and his pity for John and Jonathan, stillborn in New Canaan, his Concord neighbors whose imprisoning, delegated functions have barred them from "the only true America." Insofar as his attitude toward them follows his westward walk, it may be taken as a touchstone of our native cultural journey from hermeneutics to symbolism. Richard Mather regarded any deviance from the ideal with alarm; Cotton Mather palliated his despair through a schizophrenic duality of vision; Thoreau overcomes schizophrenia in the totalizing aesthetic security of the symbol. That actually he engaged in politics, with growing alarm and despair, only underscores his place in our literary tradition, as a romantic artist whose work is rendered distinctive by its uniquely American use of the national image. More precisely, the discrepancy between Thoreau's politics and his art underscores the uniqueness of the literary strategy by which he celebrates himself as the representative America—with Hester, Pierre, Whitman, and the Emersonian scholar a symbolist become the inclusive image of America.

The Colonial Experience
in the Literature of the United States

by Kenneth B. Murdock

It is often said, especially by foreign critics of our culture, that American literature has suffered and still suffers from our lack of a "literary tradition." Just what "tradition" means in this context is a complicated question.[1] I believe, however, that it is possible to maintain that certain themes, attitudes, and methods recur often enough in American writing to entitle them to be called "traditional." Indeed it seems to be possible that we have not one but several "traditions," as most national literatures have, and that it is the interaction of "traditions," not the exclusive dominance of one, that gives a special "American" flavor to some of our best books. The "traditional" material made use of in these books may not differ basically from the "traditional" in other literatures but there seems to me to be often a difference of emphasis, a greater weighting by American artists of certain themes, symbols, and images than is given to them by most artists elsewhere. And I should like to suggest that the special American emphases are in part, although only in part, the product of the historical experience of dwellers in this country before as well as after the United States came into existence.

No serious student of American literature neglects its English and European relationships or disregards the extent to which it

[1]For various uses of the word "tradition," see Harry Levin, The tradition of tradition, *The Hopkins Review* 4: 5-14, Spring, 1951.

has been shaped in various periods by contemporaneous events in local history or by specific aspects of the author's immediate environment. But I think we too often forget the possible literary effects of what I have called "the colonial experience"—the experience of European and English settlers here before, say, 1789. This experience gradually led many of them to think of the New World, not the Old, as their home and drew the various colonies together in a consciousness of some common interests, beliefs, and aims. Even though they kept their political allegiances abroad, the colonists often became emotionally "Americans," and some of the writers among them did their best to express their emotion. Their work displayed ways of feeling and thought which were to be kept alive among those who later built the new nation and tried to give literary expression to its ways of life, its aspirations, and its codes of value. The writing of the colonial period is often imitative, but some of it has a quality, a characteristic emphasis, which makes it recognizably "American." Its best pages, some of which interested Lamb, Southey, Voltaire, Chateaubriand, and other foreign readers and are still worth reading, reveal facets of the "colonial experience" or, it might be more accurate to say, the "colonial state of mind."

That "state of mind" was complex but some of its elements are easily isolated. Captain John Smith, one of the founders of Virginia, was a patriotic Englishman who never dreamed of independence for the colonies, but he combined with his loyalty to his native country an enthusiastic devotion to the "plantations" here, which he called, "My Wife, my Hawks, Hounds, my Cards, my Dice, and in totall, my best Content."[2] Smith's experience in the New World not only stimulated a love for "plantations" but also developed some ways of thinking which were shared by many other colonists and eventually provided good material for literature in the United States. Smith did not like taking orders from the Virginia Company in London and was contemptuous of stay-at-homes who had no taste for heroic adventuring in America. He ascribed to pioneering a kind of moral value and to the

[2] *Travels and works of Captain John Smith*, ed. Edward Arber and A. C. Bradley, 2: 770, Edinburgh, J. Grant, 1910.

pioneer a special brand of heroism. He respected birth and breeding but he saw plainly that in Virginia there was less need for gentlemen than for soldiers and good workmen. There were in the colony chances for them to acquire land, a measure of prosperity, and eventually some social prestige—in other words to become "self-made men." In the literature of the United States special value has often been given to the "self-made man" or to the man who is in some sense a pioneer and often rebellious toward any authority which seems to hamper his independent enterprise.[3] And in the same literature prowess with an ax, a plow, or a rifle has often been used as a better measure of human value than a title or a position in aristocratic society. The "self-made man" is not of course an American creation—the legend of Dick Whittington attests to that—but Franklin's *Autobiography* is perhaps the classic literary portrait of the type.[4] Nor were the heroic and rebellious pioneer and the good workman, given prestige and dignity by his skill, invented in the New World. But the American colonial experience gave special opportunities for the expert workman, the independent pioneer, and the "self-made man" to prove themselves.[5] Naturally their virtues were celebrated; naturally they have continued to appear as heroic types in the political and social folklore as well as in the literature of the United States.

Beside them stand two other heroic figures important in Amer-

[3]Irvin G. Wyllie, *The self-made man in America: the myth of rags to riches*, 6, New Brunswick, N.J., Rutgers Univ. Press, 1954, maintains that "the legendary hero of America is the self-made man." The book is concerned primarily with the post-colonial period and with men whose success was economic but it offers suggestive material for the study of the colonial "self-made man," who sometimes achieved quasi-heroic status by his physical prowess and his ability to conquer the wilderness and extend the area of settlement, even though in so doing he did not win great material rewards. Cooper's Natty Bumpo is a heroic "self-made" man albeit not rich. Hemingway's heroes, rich or not, are often heroic chiefly by virtue of the sort of physical skill which helped to make the colonial settlers of the wilderness successful.

[4]On the English background of the "self-made man," see Wyllie, *op. cit.*, 10-11. Franklin, Mr. Wyllie says (*idem*, 13) was the "first object of adoration in this cult [of the self-made man] , the convenient symbol which linked the success traditions of" the eighteenth and nineteenth centuries.

[5]*Idem*, 11.

ican mythology—the spiritual pioneer and the farmer. Both began to be celebrated in the colonial period; both are still living symbols for most of us. The colonial ancestry of one goes back to the Puritan, a pilgrim and a pioneer hoping to build a new commonwealth of God in the wilderness. A colonial author said that one Puritan leader in the early days of Massachusetts "would put a King in his Pocket"[6]—a succinct statement of the Puritan's willingness to defy any human authority which lacked divine sanction. The farmer hero, too, who reappears again and again in our literature, traces his ancestry back to the colonial period. According to Hector St. John de Crèvecoeur, a farmer and colonist writing about 1775, the American is by definition the farmer; we are "a people of cultivators." The American is "a new man, who acts upon new principles" and can do so because his farm gives him freedom.[7] The image of the American tiller of the soil as happy, virtuous, and free was far older than Crèvecoeur. In 1670 Daniel Denton wrote that in New York people lived "blest with Peace and plenty" in farm houses "begirt with Hives of Bees," and scorned "those parts of the world" which were cursed with "pride and oppression." In New York "a Waggon or Cart" gave "as good content as a Coach" and "a piece of...home-made Cloth" was "better than the finest Lawns or richest Silks." Its houses "shut their doors against pride and luxury," yet stood "wide open" in charity to the stranger.[8] In 1955 New York may not be conspicuous for homespun garments, agrarian virtue, or charity to strangers, but even in 1956 and even in New York I suspect that the hearts of countless men and women cling to the myth in spite of the actuality. The farmer and his blessed state still live in the "deep well" of the unconscious[9] and produce

[6]Cotton Mather, *Magnalia Christi Americana*, Bk. 3, Part 1, Appendix, Section 20, London, 1702.

[7]Crèvecoeur, *Letters from an American farmer*, ed. W. B. Blake, 40, 44, 67-68, N. Y., Everyman's Library, n.d.

[8]Daniel Denton, *A brief description of New York*, 19, 20, London, 1670.

[9]Henry James used the phrase "the deep well of unconscious cerebration" in his preface to *The American* in *Works* ("New York Edition"), 2: vii. John L. Lowes, *The road to Xanadu*, 54-63, Boston, Houghton Mifflin, 1927, discusses this "well," in the sense in which the word is used in this paper, as an element in the process of artistic creation.

peculiar sentimentalities, erratic behavior, frustrations, and daring dreams in men to whom on the conscious level the word "farmer" is a term of derision.[10]

Another aspect of the "colonial experience," which had significant literary consequences was the colonists' falling in love with the land. Their affection for it might be based on its practical and material value or, as among the Puritans, on a vision of it as a partial revelation of God. There also developed early the romantic notion that the space and beauty of the continent meant that it was a providentially created setting for a new race of heroes. The unexplored areas to the west stimulated dreams. Somewhere beyond the Appalachians might be a "passage to India," "the garden of the world," a land of special rewards for the courageous pioneer or the pious Pilgrim. "The West as Symbol and Myth" during the nineteenth century has been well studied by Professor Henry Nash Smith, but we should remember that the creation of both the myth and the symbol began well before 1800.[11]

For most colonists, however, the imagined glory of the West was less intimately moving than their immediate environment. The woods they cleared and the fields they tilled within sight and sound of the Atlantic aroused almost at once passionate devotion. Captain John Smith asserted that Virginia was more pleasant for "habitation" than "the most pleasant places of *Europe, Asia*" or "*Africa*" and that "heaven and earth never agreed better to frame a place" for man to live in.[12] The colonists' love for their environment, their curiosity about it, and the excitement with which they explored and settled the American wilderness surely helped to account for Thoreau's later glorification of the "wild," for the special symbolic role that the Mississippi has played in our literature,

[10]There may be a relation between the legendary heroism of the "self-made man" and that of the farmer. Wyllie, *op. cit.,* 24, 27, says that "along with the glorification of poverty" from which the "self-made man" starts "went the glorification of rural childhood. ... It would be difficult to say how many farmers' sons...won fame and fortune but there is little doubt that contemporaries" in the post-colonial period "exaggerated their number."

[11]Henry N. Smith, *Virgin land, The American West as symbol and myth,* 13, 121, Cambridge, Harvard Univ. Press, 1950.

[12]*Travels and works of Captain John Smith* 1: 48.

for our fellow-feeling for Huckleberry Finn when he prefers his raft or his barrel to the widow's house in the village, and for the symbols we find central in a story like Faulkner's *The Bear*.

To list the dozens of American authors whose work, compared to that done abroad, shows a special emphasis on the American natural environment and on the types of heroic character which were most significant in the "colonial experience" would be tedious. My contention is not that this "experience" was the only, or even the most important, source of symbols, myths, evocative images, and definitions of human value used by many contributors to the literature of the United States, but simply that it was one source, vigorously reinforced by later experiences during the period of westward expansion, which has given the American artist a body of traditional material useful in his work, however modern his theme or however slight his explicit concern with the American past.

Two examples must suffice. Sinclair Lewis's *Arrowsmith*, one of his strongest novels, is the story of a scientist, pioneering in medical research with all the fervor of a colonial frontiersman moving westward. The tone of the book is set in the opening paragraphs, which describe a girl driving a wagon through the "forest and swamp of the Ohio wilderness." Urged to seek shelter she cries "We're going on jus' long as we can. Going West! They's a whole lot of new things I aim to be seeing." "That," Mr. Lewis tells us, "was the great-grandmother of Martin Arrowsmith."[13] The image of the girl's eager pilgrimage is evocative because from the earliest days of settlement the pioneer, the man free to push westward in order to see new things and able to master his environment by his own skill, has been a heroic figure. No one need suppose, of course, that Mr. Lewis ever spent hours reading the narratives of the colonists or even the novels of Cooper. His sense of the validity of the myth probably came from a strain of feeling established so firmly by a set of environmental and historical conditions that it is the common property of hundreds and thousands of Americans who understand little or nothing of its background.

[13]Sinclair Lewis, *Arrowsmith,* 1, N.Y., Harcourt, Brace, 1925.

Or, take as another example, Arthur Miller's play, *The Death
of a Salesman*. In this country the play was a popular success and
was also enthusiastically acclaimed by the critics. It told the story
of a traveling salesman in contemporary New York, forced to
recognize that he was old and a failure. What is significant for my
purposes is that Mr. Miller presented his unhappy hero and
dramatized his plight largely in terms of symbols from the mythology which the colonial experience helped to construct. The
symbols no longer correspond as they once did to the concrete
realities of American life; their appeal is probably to a nostalgia,
to a primitive desire for escape from cruel actuality into a better
world which is believed in because of the legend that it was once
realized or nearly enough realized to make it for many Americans
a compelling source of action.

Mr. Miller's salesman, Willy Loman, facing failure, is increasingly given to recurrent reveries centered on life among trees and
flowers, outside the city, where he has a chance to live by the labor
of his hands close to the soil. One of his sons is an outspoken rebel
against the town. "With a ranch," he says, "I could do the work I
like and still be something." The salesman's brother, Ben, has
started for Alaska and ultimately found riches in Africa. He is the
American pioneer, translated from the age of settlement to the
twentieth century. His unsuccessful brother admires him and
thinks of him walking down "some open road." Willy himself
yearns despairingly for his childhood when he sat under a wagon
in Nebraska and Ben picked flowers for him. He proudly remem-
bers his father who drove his team "right across the country."
Hemmed in by city walls, he dreams of hunting and urges his
sons to "walk into a jungle" as their uncle Ben did. When at last
he can go on no longer Willy commits suicide, but only after he
has cried despairingly that he has nothing "in the ground" and
has feverishly tried to plant a garden.[14] That American audiences
sympathized with Willy Loman and felt him to be pathetic, or
even tragic (and that English critics were often cool toward the
play) suggests to me that the symbols by means of which his frus-
tration was expressed were in 1949 still real to Americans, still
part of their mythology. And that mythology, if I am right, has

[14]Miller, *Death of a salesman*, 26, 47, 48, 49, 122, 125, N.Y., Viking, 1950.

some of its roots at least in the experience of the seventeenth and eighteenth century colonists in this country.

I do not suggest for a moment that an American author's use of the "colonial experience" is in any sense a measure of the artistic value of his work. My suggestion is simply that the "colonial experience" is the source of something which can be without too much straining called a "literary tradition" — a traditional belief in certain values and certain types of character, certain symbols and their implications. For better or for worse this belief has been given artistic expression by generations of American writers who have reiterated and affirmed it. It has affected others, too, who have not been interested in it as an article of faith but who have been to some extent directed by it toward metaphors and images which are effective for American audiences because they are rooted in an American mythology. Still others, ostensibly in full protest against the old values, write with an obvious consciousness of the strength of the tradition. It remains powerful even when it is rebelled against.[15] From Thoreau and Emerson to E. A. Robinson and Robert Frost; from Nathaniel Hawthorne to Henry James and William Faulkner; from Cooper to Hemingway or Washington Irving to James Russell Lowell; from Benjamin Franklin to Mark Twain or Sinclair Lewis, American literary history supports the point.

The tradition derived from the "colonial experience" is certainly not the only force of its kind which has influenced the American artist. But it seems probable that it, together with other elements in our cultural background, must be understood if the critic is fully to comprehend the nature and method of scores of American books. In a time when thorough and perceptive criticism, based on full investigation of the artistic process is greatly

[15]Delmore Schwartz, The fiction of Ernest Hemingway, *Perspectives U.S.A.*, 13: 87, quotes Hemingway: "A country was made to be as we found it. Our people went to America because that was the place to go then." But they made a "bloody mess of it" and Hemingway turned to Africa: "I knew a good country when I saw one. Here there was game, plenty of birds....Here I could hunt and fish." Mr. Schwartz comments: "The pioneer and the immigrant and the hunter and fisherman are identical in the Hemingway hero whenever he thinks of how to regain the dream" which is "formulated in the American Constitution as every human being's inalienable right to life, liberty, and the pursuit of happiness."

needed, we cannot afford to neglect, as much as most American literary histories and anthologies have done, the thought, feeling, and literary expression of those who, in the first one hundred and seventy-five years of English and European settlement on these shores, set patterns in which some artists are still able to find stimulus for the imagination.

Chronology of Important Dates

1607	First permanent English settlement established at Jamestown. John Smith gives a brief account of the colony in *A True Relation of Virginia* (published in London in 1608).
1617	Establishment of the Virginia House of Burgesses, the first representative assembly in America.
1620	Founding of Plymouth Colony. William Bradford recounts the history of the Pilgrim colonists in *Of Plymouth Plantation* (not published until 1897).
1630	The Puritans settle Massachusetts Bay. John Winthrop begins his *Journal*, first published in 1825-26 as *The History of New England from 1630 to 1649*.
1636-37	The Antinomian crisis. Anne Hutchinson banished from Massachusetts Bay.
1640	Civil War in England.
1644	Roger Williams secures a charter for Rhode Island from Parliament and publishes *The Bloudy Tenent of Persecution*.
1653	Edward Johnson, *Wonder-Working Providence*.
1655	Anne Bradstreet, *The Tenth Muse, lately Sprung up in America*.
1660	Restoration of Charles II.
1662	The Halfway Covenant adopted by the New England churches, liberalizing standards for admission.
1676	Bacon's Rebellion in Virginia.
1681	William Penn founds the colony of Pennsylvania.
1682	Mary Rowlandson, *The Soveraignty and Goodness of God*. Edward Taylor writes the first of his *Preparatory Meditations* (discovered in 1937 and first published in 1939).

1693   Cotton Mather's defense of the Salem witch trials, *The Wonders of the Invisible World.*

1702   Cotton Mather, *Magnalia Christi Americana.*

1705   Robert Beverley, *The History and Present State of Virginia.*

ca. 1732   William Byrd II begins *The History of the Dividing Line* (not published until 1841).

1739-42   The religious revival known as the Great Awakening sweeps through the colonies.

1746   Jonathan Edwards, *A Treatise concerning Religious Affections.*

1756   England and France at war.

1757   Benjamin Franklin, *The Way to Wealth.*

1758   Edwards, *The Great Christian Doctrine of Original Sin Defended.*

1763   Treaty of Paris ends the Seven Years War and establishes British hegemony over North America.

1765   Parliament passes the Stamp Act, provoking protests throughout the colonies. John Adams, *A Dissertation on the Canon and Feudal Law.*

1771   Franklin begins his *Autobiography.*

1774   Thomas Jefferson, *A Summary View of the Rights of British America. Journal* of John Woolman.

1775   Battle of Concord and Lexington.

1776   Declaration of Independence adopted by the Second Continental Congress, July 4. Publication of Thomas Paine's *Common Sense* and the first of his pamphlets on *The American Crisis* ("These are the times that try men's souls.").

1782   Hector St. John de Crèvecoeur, *Letters from an American Farmer.*

1783   Treaty of Paris signed, ending the Revolutionary conflict.

1786   Philip Freneau, *Poems.* Shays's Rebellion breaks out in western Massachusetts.

1787   First English edition of Jefferson's *Notes on the State of Virginia.* First number of the *Federalist Papers.*

1788   Ratification of the Constitution.

1791   Creation of the Bank of the United States.

1792   Hugh Henry Brackenridge, Volume I of *Modern Chivalry.*

1798   Charles Brockden Brown publishes *Wieland,* the first of his four major novels.

1800   Jefferson's election. Second Great Awakening. Publication of Brown's *Arthur Mervyn,* Volume II.

Notes on the Editor and Contributors

MICHAEL T. GILMORE, the editor, teaches at Brandeis University. He is the author of *The Middle Way: Puritanism and Ideology in American Romantic Fiction* (1977) and has also edited *Twentieth Century Interpretations of Moby-Dick.*

MICHAEL DAVITT BELL, who teaches at Williams College, is the author of *Hawthorne and the Historical Romance of New England* (1971).

SACVAN BERCOVITCH is Professor of English and Comparative Literature at Columbia University. He has written numerous essays and books on early American literature, including *The Puritan Origins of the American Self* (1975) and *The American Jeremiad* (1978).

URSULA BRUMM, author of *American Thought and Religious Typology* (1970), teaches at the Free University of Berlin. She is the European editor of the journal *Early American Literature.*

ROBERT DALY is Associate Professor of English at the State University of New York at Buffalo and the author of *God's Altar: The World and the Flesh in Puritan Poetry* (1978).

ERIC FONER teaches history at the City College of New York. His books include *Free Soil, Free Labor, Free Men: The Ideology of the Republican Party before the Civil War* (1970).

PERRY MILLER was Powell M. Cabot Professor of American Literature at Harvard University until his death in 1963. His monumental studies of *The New England Mind* transformed contemporary understanding of Puritanism.

KENNETH B. MURDOCK, who was Miller's colleague at Harvard, published several important works on the Puritans, including a biography of *Increase Mather* (1925).

EDWIN C. ROZWENC was Chairman of the Department of American Studies at Amherst College and the editor of a number of volumes in the "Amherst series" of *Problems in American Civilization.*

ROBERT F. SAYRE is Professor of English at the University of Iowa. His most recent book is *Thoreau and the American Indians* (1977).

KENNETH SILVERMAN, author of *A Cultural History of the American Revolution* (1976), is Professor of English at New York University. He is currently preparing a biography of Cotton Mather.

LEWIS P. SIMPSON is the William A. Read Professor of English at Louisiana State University and co-editor of *The Southern Review.* His books include *The Man of Letters in New England and the South* (1973).

RICHARD SLOTKIN, author of *Regeneration Through Violence* (1973), is Professor of English and American Studies at Wesleyan University.

GARRY WILLS is Adjunct Professor of Humanities at the Johns Hopkins University. He has published widely on American culture and history and is the author of *Nixon Agonistes* (1970).

Selected Bibliography

It is beyond the scope of this volume to provide a comprehensive bibliography of scholarship on early American literature. For more extensive bibliographical surveys the reader is urged to consult the following works: Sacvan Bercovitch, ed., *The American Puritan Imagination: Essays in Revaluation* (New York: Cambridge Univ. Press, 1974); Richard Beale Davis, *American Literature Through Bryant,* Goldentree Bibliographies in Language and Literature (New York: Appleton-Century-Crofts, 1969); Everett Emerson, ed., *Major Writers of Early American Literature* (Madison: Univ. of Wisconsin Press, 1972) and *American Literature, 1764-1789: The Revolutionary Years* (Madison: Univ. of Wisconsin Press, 1977); David Levin and Theodore L. Gross, eds., *America in Literature,* Vol. I (New York: John Wiley & Sons, 1978); and Robert A. Rees and Earl N. Harbert, eds., *Fifteen American Authors Before 1900: Bibliographic Essays on Research and Criticism* (Madison: Univ. of Wisconsin Press, 1971). Relevant journals include the *William and Mary Quarterly* and *Early American Literature.* Listed below are a few important studies on the period, with emphasis on items that have appeared since 1965.

Bailyn, Bernard. *The Ideological Origins of the American Revolution.* Cambridge, Mass.: Harvard Univ. Press, 1967.

Bercovitch, Sacvan. *The American Jeremiad.* Madison: Univ. of Wisconsin Press, 1978.

————. *The Puritan Origins of the American Self.* New Haven, Conn.: Yale Univ. Press, 1975.

Davis, Richard Beale. *Intellectual Life in the Colonial South, 1585-1763.* 3 vols. Knoxville: Univ. of Tennessee Press, 1978.

Elliott, Emory. *Power and the Pulpit in Puritan New England.* Princeton: Princeton Univ. Press, 1975.

Gelpi, Albert. *The Tenth Muse: The Psyche of the American Poet.* Cambridge, Mass.: Harvard Univ. Press, 1975.

Granger, Bruce. *American Essay Serials from Franklin to Irving.* Knoxville: Univ. of Tennessee Press, 1978.

Heimert, Alan. *Religion and the American Mind: From the Great Awakening to the Revolution.* Cambridge, Mass.: Harvard Univ. Press, 1966.

Jones, Howard Mumford. *O Strange New World. American Culture: The Formative Years.* New York: The Viking Press, 1964.

Kolodny, Annette. *The Lay of the Land: Metaphor as Experience and History in American Life and Letters.* Chapel Hill: Univ. of North Carolina Press, 1975.

Leary, Lewis, *Soundings: Some Early American Writers.* Athens: Univ. of Georgia Press, 1975.

Lemay, J. A. Leo. *Men of Letters in Colonial Maryland.* Knoxville: Univ. of Tennessee Press, 1972.

Levin, David. *Cotton Mather: The Young Life of the Lord's Remembrancer, 1663-1703.* Cambridge, Mass.: Harvard Univ. Press, 1978.

Martin, Terence. *The Instructed Vision: Scottish Common Sense Philosophy and the Origins of American Fiction.* Bloomington: Indiana Univ. Press, 1961.

Marx, Leo. *The Machine in the Garden: Technology and the Pastoral Ideal in America.* New York: Oxford Univ. Press, 1964.

May, Henry F. *The Enlightenment in America.* New York: Oxford Univ. Press, 1976.

Miller, Perry. *Errand into the Wilderness.* Cambridge, Mass.: Harvard Univ. Press, 1956.

———. *The New England Mind: The Seventeenth Century.* Cambridge, Mass.: Harvard Univ. Press, 1939.

———. *The New England Mind: From Colony to Province.* Cambridge, Mass.: Harvard Univ. Press, 1953.

Pocock, J. G. A. *The Machiavellian Moment: Florentine Political Thought and the Atlantic Republican Tradition.* Princeton: Princeton Univ. Press, 1975.

Scheick, William J. *The Will and the Word: The Poetry of Edward Taylor.* Athens: Univ. of Georgia Press, 1974.

Seelye, John. *Prophetic Waters: The River in Early American Life and Literature.* New York: Oxford Univ. Press, 1977.

Shea, Daniel B., Jr. *Spiritual Autobiography in Early America.* Princeton: Princeton Univ. Press, 1968.

Stourzh, Gerald. *Alexander Hamilton and the Idea of Republican Government.* Stanford, Calif.: Stanford Univ. Press, 1970.

Tichi, Cecilia. *New World, New Earth: Environmental Reform in American Literature from the Puritans through Whitman.* New Haven, Conn.: Yale University Press, 1979.

Tuveson, Ernest Lee. *Redeemer Nation: The Idea of America's Millennial Role.* Chicago: Univ. of Chicago Press, 1968.

Wood, Gordon S. *The Creation of the American Republic, 1776-1787.* Chapel Hill: Univ. of North Carolina Press, 1969.

Wright, Louis B. *The Cultural Life of the American Colonies, 1607-1763.* New York: Harper, 1957.

Ziff, Larzer. *Puritanism in America: New Culture in a New World.* New York: The Viking Press, 1973.